A River Runner's Guide

Guide

— to the —

History

of the

GRAND CANYON

Kim Crumbo

JOHNSON BOOKS: BOULDER

In memory of
Lois Brooks Webster

Fourth Printing 1994
ISBN 0-933472-61-7
Library of Congress Catalog Card No.: 81-84310

Cover design by Margaret Donharl
Maps by Llyn French
Illustration on page 16 by Mesia Simonds
Photographs courtesy of
   Grand Canyon National Park Study Collection

Printed in the United States of America by
Johnson Printing Company
1880 South 57th Court
Boulder, Colorado 80301

Mr. Kim Crumbo has put together a handy little book here, one which will serve nicely as a companion and supplement to Buzz Belknap's *Grand Canyon River Guide*. Crumbo's book goes more into details of the history of river-running in Grand Canyon, with much information not heretofore available in one compact edition. Both books should be a standard part of the Grand Canyon river-runner's ammo box library.

I have read Belknap's book over and over again, as an easy way of partly reliving the Canyon river trip; Crumbo's book will no doubt come to provide a similar pleasure for many river-trippers of the future. Everything in it is immensely interesting to all who participate in a Canyon voyage, probably because, being human, we find the natural scene too strange and overwhelming to be fully comprehended and enjoyed for its own sake alone.

We seek the human touch here and there. The ruins of a cabin, the traces of a foot path, the wreckage of an old boat, the ancient artifacts and rock art of the aboriginal explorers lend an extra dimension to our enjoyment, giving us details we can understand within a scale we can grasp. Our sympathy with these evidences of human history makes the natural history beyond and beneath it seem all the more grand, vast, mysterious and beautiful. Something most of our scenic photographers and painters fail to understand, for example, is that a lone human figure in the foreground, or even an animal with human associations such as a horse, or a dead cow, or a mummified tourist stranded on a ledge, sets off the background by dramatic contrast, enhancing as a whole the sublime wonder of the Canyon landscape.

Certain human touches, on the other hand, do not help. The prevalence of airplanes and helicopters in and above the Grand Canyon is a distracting, irritating nuisance which should no longer be tolerated by anybody.

Meanwhile—the great Canyon endures. The Canyon endures the trifling busyness of humans as it does the industry of ants, the trickle-down erosion of snow and freeze, the cascade of floods, the transient insult of Glen Canyon Dam. These things shall pass, the Canyon will outlive them all. The grandeur of the Canyon confers dignity on every form of life within its walls, even down unto the meanest and the most petty. It is an honor to be a visitor in the Grand Canyon of the Colorado, as it is an honor and a privilege to be alive, however briefly, on this marvelous planet we call Earth.

Long live the wilderness!

Edward Abbey
Wolf Hole, Arizona

The Colorado River is renowned for its white-   **Introduction**
water, as it should be. Rapids are important, every-
one tells me. They get us wet, frighten us a little or
a lot, and occasionally humiliate us. Rapids give us
stories to tell and embellish. God bless them.

But the River is more than rapids. The River is
magic. It swirls and flows to carry our boat or hearts
where we may or may not wish to go. The River is
silence interrupted by obvious cataracts or unseen
currents suddenly boiling to the surface. It is the
peaceful morning breeze or a howling wind. The
River is merely our response to the magic of water
flowing through the most beautiful place on earth.

The following text recounts a sampling of human-
ity's encounter with the wild Colorado River. Following the River's chronology, events are tied to
places in a mile-by-mile sequence for reference. The
text is keyed to the maps that follow. Miles below
Lee's Ferry are marked on the maps and in the mar-
gin of the text. This guidebook is offered with the
hope that an awareness of the words, emotions, and
actions of earlier canyon folks will enhance your
Grand Canyon experience.

I could not have completed this guidebook without the encouragement and assistance of many good
people. Thank you Randy Stutman, Curt Sauer, Bob

Euler, P. T. Reilly, George Billingsly, and Jan Balsom for your guidance, patience, and information. A special thanks to Ken Sleight who brought me to the Canyon and left me there, and Stu Reeder whose advice and example helped me survive those first few years. And thanks, Ed, wherever you are. Someday, somehow Grand Canyon will again mean clear skies, natural quiet, wild rivers, and wolves on the rim.

Long live the wilderness!

In the winter of 1776, a lost, tired, and starving group of travelers, led by Franciscan Fathers Silvestre Velez de Escalante and Francisco Atanasio Dominguez, arrived at a place surrounded by red cliffs, which they named San Benito Salispuedes (meaning "get out if you can"). To survive, they killed one of their horses for food. The fathers' search for a route between Santa Fe and Monterey, California, had taken them on a long, circuitous journey through northern Utah and then south again. Early snows forced them to this spot as they attempted to return to Santa Fe.

Mile 0.0
Escalante
Map 1

After three days of searching for a way out of this cul de sac, the party decided on a difficult route two miles up the Rio de Santa Teresa (now the Paria River). The party spent three hours climbing a steep incline they call "Las Animas." They reached the summit of the Paria Plateau and proceeded northward to Glen Canyon. Ultimately they found a ford at a place now remembered as El Vado de los Padres, the Crossing of the Fathers.

**John Wesley
Powell**

Nearly a century passed before the first river expedition arrived at Salispuedes, the mouth of the Paria. On August 4, 1869, after a long day spent battling headwinds that resembled a "perfect tornado with lightning and rain," three boats pulled in for camp. Major John Wesley Powell led this party of nine ragged men on what was the first expedition down the canyons of the Green and Colorado rivers.

John Wesley Powell

Powell had served as a Union Officer in the Civil War, an ordeal which earned him the title "Major" and cost him his right forearm in the Battle of Shiloh. Powell organized the expedition for scientific purposes, but a series of accidents and equipment losses and a critical food shortage turned the affair into a survival ordeal. By the time they reached the Paria, the crew had traveled nearly 600 miles of river and endured many hardships. Their most formidable obstacle, the Grand Canyon, still lay before them.

John D. Lee and Lee's Ferry

The first settler at the mouth of the Paria, a Mormon named John Doyle Lee, arrived in December 1871. Lee's presence in this desolate place (called "Lonely Dell" by his wife) was not entirely his choosing. As a result of his participation in the 1857 Mountain Meadow Massacre, the gruesome Utah murders of members of a non-Mormon party, Lee emerged as the principle scapegoat. Following his excommunication from the Mormon Church, Lee was directed by Mormon leader Brigham Young to resettle at the envisioned ferry crossing at the mouth of the Paria.

During the ferry's first year of operation, customers were scarce and Lee's Ferry lacked a ferryboat. Earlier in 1870, Powell's crew had built a flat-bottomed scow to provide access across the river. When Lee's first customers appeared, a party of fifteen Navajos, he quickly repaired the *Canyon Maid* and carried the Indians across.

Lee's stay at the Paria was short-lived. In 1874, while visiting one of his wives, he was arrested in Panguitch, Utah. The courts found Lee guilty of the Mountain Meadow murders and his execution took place at Mountain Meadow, Utah, in March 1877. In spite of—or perhaps because of—Lee's notoriety, the crossing became known as Lee's Ferry.

✕

Lee's Backbone   Almost directly across the river from the Lee's Ferry boat ramp, the buff-colored Shinurump Conglomerate forms a sloping bedrock cliff. This is the infamous Lee's Backbone, a tortuous route of boulders and incised gullies that confronted early travelers. Immediately below the Shinurump and continuing downstream are the eroded remains of a road carved into the brown Moenkopi shales. This is the Long Dugway, built in 1898-99 to bypass the difficult Lee's Backbone. When maintained, the dugway allowed the passage of one wagon or automobile.

The Navajo People   The left bank of Marble Canyon, from Lee's Ferry to the Little Colorado, belongs to the Navajo people. From their home in western Canada, the ancestral Navajo traveled southward, probably along the high plains east of the Rocky Mountains. Their arrival in northwestern New Mexico occurred somewhat earlier than the seventeenth-century Spanish explorations of the same area. Through contact with tribes along the plains, as well as with the Pueblo people, these Athapascan-speaking people we call the Navajo and Apache acquired the rudiments of agriculture and pottery making. By the time of European contact, the Navajo were already a pastoral and agriculture people, living in scattered communities.

The ancestral Navajo remained restricted to northern New Mexico. Here they developed an effective economy based on traditional hunting, gathering, and agriculture, as well as raiding and herding. Agriculture provided the Navajo with maize, squash, and beans, and sheepraising gave them a dependable protein base not available to other southwestern Indians.

White-Navajo contact began in the winter of 1846 when the United States launched its first military expedition against the Navajo. In 1848, the Treaty of Guadalupe Hidalgo transferred New Mexico to the

United States. Later, taking advantage of U.S. preoccupation with the Civil War, the Navajo increased their raids on the Rio Grande settlements. They paid dearly for their plunder. In the spring of 1863, Colonel Kit Carson launched a systematic search-and-destroy effort aimed at Navajo orchards, fields, and livestock. The tactic succeeded in subduing the Navajo, most of whom surrendered and were subjected to the 330-mile "Long Walk" to Fort Sumner. A number of Navajo sought refuge in the depths of the Grand Canyon and in other inaccessible areas.

After their release in 1868, the Navajo returned to their homeland. Beginning in 1878, accessions greatly enlarged their reservation. The areas bordering the Colorado River were added between 1900 and 1930. Today, the Navajo constitute the largest single unified Native American group. Their reservation of about 25,000 square miles is roughly the size of West Virginia.

Below the Paria riffle an obvious trail cut through the Kaibab Limestone cliff appears on the left. This is the Lower Ferry Dugway, used during periods of low water from 1878 until 1896, when a permanent track cable was installed at the upper ferry site above the present launch ramp. The lower site, impossible to use during high water, allowed the traveler to bypass Lee's Backbone.

Mile 1.5
Lower Ferry Dugway
Map 1

Below Mile 4 stands the most conspicuous man-made feature between Lee's Ferry and Lake Mead. Navajo Bridge, over 450 feet above the river, established an important, dependable link between Arizona and Utah by replacing the accident-prone Lee's Ferry. In 1937, Buzz Holmstrum, the first man to intentionally run the Grand Canyon alone, stopped here for supplies. Buzz floated the river from

Mile 4.5
Navajo Bridge
Map 1

Green River, Wyoming, and after a quick but inadequate look at his map, expected an easy stroll from the river at Navajo Bridge to Marble Canyon Lodge. The 400-foot escarpment came as quite a jolt. On the left, a quarter of a mile upstream, Buzz completed an "awful climb" out of the canyon, purchased his supplies, and returned to the river at Mile 4.1.

Mile 8.0
Badger Rapid
Map 1

Along its 280-mile course through the Grand Canyon, the Colorado River drops approximately 2,200 feet in elevation. Although rapids make up less than 10 percent of the horizontal distance, they account for more than 50 percent of the vertical descent. Occasional flood waters from steeply inclined tributaries transport large boulders and great quantities of other debris into the Colorado, forming a partial dam across the river. A rapid is created as the constricted flow rumbles over the dam.

Boaters confronted with a vigorous rapid have at least four options. The first, most tempting, alternative involves burning the boat and walking out. The second option is to portage, which requires carrying equipment and boats around the dreaded cataract. This approach is safe, assuming no one is crushed beneath a dropped boat or breaks a leg as heavy gear is carried over slippery, rattlesnake-infested boulders. Lining, or let-down, is the third alternative. By using lines controlled from shore, a boat can be moved slowly and carefully along the bank until the perceived danger is passed. This method is faster and easier than portage, but some rapids are difficult, if not impossible, to line. Often this unfortunate fact is realized midway through the rapid as swift current hopelessly pins the boat against immovable rocks. Barring disaster, the fourth option, running the rapid, is usually the quickest.

Early explorers routinely lined or portaged Badger and Soap Creek Rapids, the latter being the most notorious. In 1929, Clyde Eddy, leading an expedition of "3 stout boats, eleven men, a bear and a dog," departed from Green River, Wyoming, for a sportsman's trip through the canyons of the Green and Colorado rivers. Arriving at a rapid he believed to be Soap Creek, Eddy wrote "I doubt if any boat in the world could have run through successfully at the level of water prevailing at that time." Although crewman Parley Galloway wanted to be the "first" man to run Soap Creek, Eddy insisted that they portage the stretch. (Parley was the son of the famous river-running pioneer, Nathaniel Galloway.) After a two-hour portage, the party continued on down the river and ran the next rapid without difficulty. Later, Eddy realized that the second rapid was the dreaded Soap Creek and the first was Badger.

According to legend, Mormon explorer Jacob Hamblin shot a badger somewhere in the upper drainage; hence the name Badger Canyon. Later, in another drainage, he boiled the creature in alkaline water. In the morning Jacob discovered that the badger's fat had not turned into breakfast, but into soap. Soap Creek enters the Colorado at Mile 11.

In July of 1889, the Brown-Stanton river survey portaged Soap Creek. At their camp near the foot of the thundering rapid, Frank Mason Brown and Robert Stanton sat and talked late into the evening. They spoke of home and the dangerous journey before them. Brown, leader of this party of eight (the third downriver expedition to enter Marble Canyon), retired to a troubled sleep filled with dreams of violent rapids and the dark canyon below. Stanton was an engineer hired by Brown to help determine the feasibility of constructing a railroad along the river from Colorado to California.

In the morning, Brown's boat departed camp first. Stanton's crew experienced minor difficulties, but

Mile 11.2
Soap Creek Rapid
Map 2

soon his boat was under way. Moments later, as he approached the next rapid, Stanton noticed a crewman running up the shore and waving both arms. The frantic man shouted, "Mr. Brown is in there!" as he pointed to the whirlpools of Mile 11.9. As Stanton's boat circled the turbulent eddy, Brown's notebook shot to the surface. The crew recovered the notebook, but they found no sign of Brown. The remainder of the day was spent gazing at the river's whirlpools while Peter Hansbrough carved the dead man's epitaph in the sandstone ledges on the left bank.

Twenty-two years later, another party entered Marble Canyon. At Soap Creek, Emery and Ellsworth Kolb, photographers intent on capturing on motion-picture film the drama of river running, pondered the many rocks on low-water Soap Creek Rapid. "Clearly there was no channel on that [the left] side," wrote Ellsworth, but "the right looked more feasible." On shore Emery wildly cranked the camera as Ellsworth bravely entered the rapid and promptly hit a rock that catapulted him into the icy November water. He managed to crawl back into the boat and thus completed this first, if slightly flawed, run of Soap Creek Rapid. Undaunted and determined to do better, Ellsworth decided to run the second boat through. As darkness approached, the clothes and equipment from the first boat were spread out on the beach to dry. Out on the river Ellsworth's boat gracefully rolled over before his frantic brother's eyes. Emery immediately jumped in the first boat and chased his hapless brother through the turbulent waters of a winterized Marble Canyon. He soon located his boat and hypothermic brother. They spent the next morning retrieving the equipment at Soap Creek, one mile upstream.

As late as the 1920s, no detailed plan and profile map of the Colorado River through the Grand Canyon existed. In 1923, under the leadership of Colonel Claude H. Birdseye, the U.S. Geological Survey launched its own map-making expedition to locate future dam sites. At Tanner Wash the expedition "reached a rapid that lay between vertical cliffs which rose directly from the water," allowing no opportunity to scout or portage. The party fearlessly splashed their way through the riffle they named "Shear Wall."

Mile 14.4
Sheer Wall Rapid
Map 2

In an upper drainage of Rider Canyon, two large rocks fallen together form a shelter. Sometime before 1871, a traveler used the low refuge and inscribed with charcoal along the top of the rock "Rock House Hotel." A nearby seep soon acquired the name House Rock Spring, and eventually House Rock Valley received its title, or so the story goes. House Rock Wash drains into Rider Canyon, which later reaches the Colorado, forming House Rock Rapid.

Mile 17.0
House Rock Rapid
Map 2

On January 2, 1890, members of Robert Stanton's second river expedition carried an injured crewman, Franklin A. Nims, up the difficult route through Rider Canyon to the rim. Nims, the expedition's photographer, had fallen from a twenty-foot cliff the day before. Unconscious, his ankle broken, Nims lay tied to a stretcher improvised from two oars and a piece of canvas. At times the pathetic cargo dangled in mid-air as the crew hauled Nims over ledges and up treacherous talus slopes. Without blankets or food, they endured a snow-filled night as they waited for Stanton to return with a wagon and driver from Lee's Ferry, 35 miles away. The wagon arrived the following morning and the eight-man crew hurriedly bid Nims farewell, "though he was unconscious," and returned to the boats, which were guarded by two crewmen fortunate enough to have missed the entire episode.

Nims awoke one week later on the floor of a Lee's Ferry farmhouse. Unknown to Nims, Stanton considered him off the payroll the moment he fell off the ledge. Nims received no reimbursement for medical or traveling expenses incurred during his six-month convalescence.

Mile 22.0
Redwall
Limestone
Map 3

On the left bank a glistening layer of river-polished limestone appears at water level. Powell assumed the rock to be marble and subsequently gave Marble Canyon its name. Further downstream, as the river cuts deeper into the gray limestone, runoff from the overlying Supai and Hermit formations stains the limestone red. Throughout the canyon this formation weathers to an imposing 500-foot cliff called the Redwall Limestone.

Mile 24.5
Bert Loper
Map 3

In the summer of 1949, two small wooden boats and an inflatable raft pulled from a lunch stop near Mile 21. Well ahead of the main party, a fourth boat, the *Grand Canyon*, carried Wayne Nichol and boatman Bert Loper toward 24.5 Mile Rapid. With the other boats behind, Nichol suggested that they pull in to inspect the approaching rapid. Loper, a 79-year-old man with a 20-year history of heart trouble, either ignored the request or was simply too exhausted to attempt the landing. Midway through the rapid the boat began to turn to one side. Nichol looked over his shoulder and shouted, "Bert, look to your oars," but Loper remained still. In an instant the boat capsized. Nichol managed to reach shore at Cave Springs Rapid as Bert, motionless and with both eyes closed, floated downstream in the turbulent river.

The remainder of that day was spent searching in vain for his body. On a rocky bar, immediately below

Bert Loper

Loper's boat and monument, now destroyed by vandals

Buck Farm Canyon, the forlorn crew found the *Grand Canyon*. The bow compartment of Bert's homemade, plywood boat was completely empty. The stern deck was badly damaged. In a sad ceremony, the small crew pulled the boat well above the highwater line, beneath a large mesquite. At the head of the *Grand Canyon*'s bow they painted this epitaph:

Bert Loper
Grand Old Man of the
Colorado
Born: July 31, 1869   Died: July 8, 1949

For twenty-six years Bert Loper's body remained concealed in the Canyon. Then in 1975, a hiker located a human skeleton at an old high-water line at Cardenas Canyon. Subsequent analysis confirmed (they say) that the bleached bones belonged to Bert Loper. Against Bert's expressed desires, his remains were hauled from his beloved river to the smog of a Salt Lake City cemetery.

Mile 24.9
**Hansbrough-
Richards Rapid**
Map 3

On the morning of July 15, 1889, disaster again struck the struggling Stanton-Brown party. Immediately after lining 25 Mile Rapid, Peter Hansbrough and Henry Richards capsized along the cliff on the left. Richards, one of the expedition's two black crewmen, attempted to swim but sank. Hansbrough was never again seen alive.

From the very beginning, the Stanton-Brown expedition seemed disaster bound. The party nearly starved in Cataract Canyon, 200 miles upstream. Their thin, brittle, and unstable cedar boats were totally inadequate for the rigors of the rapids. Well aware of the toils endured by Powell's crew of hardy frontiersmen, Stanton suggested that experienced boatmen accompany the expedition. Brown, leader of the expedition, vetoed the idea and instead invited "two charming and genial young lawyers" to handle

Boat of the Stanton Expedition, 1889-90

the boats. Stanton, a nonswimmer, suggested they use life preservers. Brown neglected to provide them, an oversight that cost three lives. With a crew too small and demoralized to continue, Stanton decided to abandon the expedition at South Canyon, Mile 32. Before beginning their sad retreat out of "death's canyon," Stanton gazed up the main stream. At that moment the muddy, rain-swollen river bid his crew one last, ghastly farewell: beyond their reach, the body of Frank Mason Brown swiftly passed downstream.

On August 6, 1923, the U.S. Geological Survey expedition arrived at the head of an "abrupt and noisy rapid" where a number of small, clear springs seeped from the canyon wall. The men discovered, half-buried in the sand of a large cave, traps, cooking utensils, a brace and bit, and other trapping and miner gear left by Frederick Tyler Barry and two others in 1888. Barry and his companions probably reached the cave by boat and then left the river for Flagstaff. The survey crew called the cataract Cave Rapid and Spring Cave Rapid, although the final map produced by the U.S. Geological Survey calls the stretch Cave Springs Rapid. The following morning an attempt to

Mile 25.5
Cave Springs Rapid
Map 3

line Cave Springs reduced their canvas boat *Mohave* to kindling. The remaining four boats ran the rapid without mishap.

Mile 29.0
Shinumo Wash
Map 4

Powell's second expedition was launched from Green River, Wyoming, in May 1871 and arrived at Lee's Ferry the following October. The boats were cached for the winter; the river expedition would resume in August. During the interlude, the party conducted a land exploration of the Grand Canyon region, including some mapping of the Kaibab Plateau. While triangulating on the high plateau, crewman Frederick Dellenbaugh occasionally took bearings on a large butte east of Marble Canyon: "It stood up so like a great altar, and, having in my mind the house building Amerinds [Pueblo] who had formerly occupied the country, and whom the Pai Utes called Shinumo, I called it Shinumo Altar." The canyon drainage north of the butte acquired the name Shinumo Wash and should not be confused with Shinumo Creek, 80 miles downstream. The National Geographic Society's 1968 expedition, which included Ron Smith and Bill Belknap, named lower Shinumo Wash's polished limestone gorge Silver Grotto.

Mile 31.8
Stanton's Cave
Map 4

Immediately downstream from South Canyon, on the right bank and 100 feet above the river, a large cave extends more than 400 feet into the Redwall. Before abandoning the river, Stanton cached his remaining supplies here. The following January, he returned on a second expedition equipped with stouter boats, adequate provisions, and life preservers. The crew found everything left in "Stanton's" Cave in good condition, except for minor rodent damage.

The men apparently overlooked one of the more intriguing aspects of the cavern. Four thousand years earlier, primitive hunters placed tiny animal figurines in the cave's dark, innermost recesses, where they remained for forty centuries. Willow twigs, split lengthwise, were wrapped and twisted until they resembled the game animals hunted by these ancient people. Often small spears pierced the figurines. The hunters probably believed these symbolic slayings insured hunting success. No one knows who these mysterious people were, but archaeologists think that this cave and many others served as shrines for hunters of the Pinto Basin-Desert Culture. The Desert Culture was a way of life practiced by prehistoric Indians who lived in the area from the Columbia River drainage to western Mexico. Archaeological remains show that they hunted large and small animals and gathered a variety of plants. They fabricated baskets, sandals, fiber nets, and grinding stones. Little else is known about these ancient people, who ceased to use their mystical Grand Canyon caves long before the Christian era.

In 1934, members of the Frazier-Eddy expedition stopped near Stanton's Cave and, to the chagrin of modern archaeologists, dug up a skeleton near the Pueblo ruins at South Canyon. Both legs of the dark-haired, buckskin-clad victim appeared broken and the skeleton "still had a bad odor to him." One crewman rummaged through a cave and found some nails, canvas, and an old gun scabbard of unknown origin. Another party member found several "little horses made of willows and sticks," and assumed them to be children's toys. Today, most of the skeleton, including the skull, and an unknown number of "toy horses" and other important archaeological artifacts are scattered across the planet.

Mile 31.0
Vasey's
Paradise
Map 4

Below Stanton's Cave a spectacular waterfall gushes from the Redwall Limestone. The springs provide moisture for a variety of water-loving plants including golden columbine, lobelia, poison ivy, and the pungent crimson monkey flower. Powell named the location Vasey's Paradise, in honor of George W. Vasey, a botanist and friend who accompanied Powell on an earlier exploration of the Rocky Mountains. Julius Stone, passing this spring in 1909, thought the waterfall to be "as enchanting as the liquid melody of a songbird." A member of Powell's second river survey in 1872 considered it "a hell of a paradise."

Mile 33.0
Redwall Cavern
Map 4

Powell discovered Redwall Cavern in 1869, and claimed it would hold 50,000 people. The cavern, though quite large, would hold 50,000 sweating bodies in the same manner a telephone booth holds eighteen.

Mile 34.8
Nautiloid
Canyon
Map 4

On the left, embedded in the limestone floor of a small canyon, are the fossil remains of several large nautiloids, squid-like animals with external shells and numerous tentacles. Though quite common during the Paleozoic, only a half-dozen species of the genus *Nautilus* survive today, dwelling in the Pacific Ocean between Fiji and the Philippines. Some ancient nautiloids, like *Rayonnoceras* found here, possessed straight, gracefully tapered cylindrical shells. Others, like the modern nautilus, have exquisitely coiled shells. Like the octopus and squid, the modern nautilus expels a jet of water through a tube-shaped funnel for locomotion. This method provides sur-

Rayonnoceras

prising mobility and quickness. Probably the many Paleozoic and Mesozoic nautiloids enjoyed a similiar free-swimming mode of life.

The river continues quietly through one of the more serene sections of Marble Canyon. The Kolb brothers, in 1911, considered this region "gloomy and prison-like," reminiscent of the dreary dungeon of Venice. They named the small natural bridge above 36 Mile Rapid "The Bridge of Sighs," recalling its likeness to the Venetian bridge where, long ago, condemned prisoners had walked from trial at Doge's Palace to the dungeon across the canal.

Mile 35.7
Bridge of Sighs
Map 4

In 1950, the Bureau of Reclamation of the Department of the Interior completed a grandiose scheme recommending, as an initial step, the construction of five major dams in the upper basin above Lee's Ferry. These proposed dams included Glen Canyon Dam on the Colorado, Navajo Dam on the San Juan, and Flaming Gorge and Echo Park dams on the Green River. Conservationists and other groups managed to kill Echo Park Dam, which directly threatened Dinosaur National Monument. Unfortunately, a 580-foot cement plug called Glen Canyon Dam was built, flooding a stunningly beautiful wilderness, Glen Canyon, and severely impacting the riverine environment of Grand Canyon.

Mile 39.5
The Dams
Map 4

By now, even the most casual observer should notice the abnormal behavior of the river. Not only is the river usually clear—not "colorado," Spanish for red—but the water level fluctuates dramatically during most twenty-four-hour periods. Both of these conditions are directly attributable to Glen Canyon Dam, a hydroelectric power station located 15 miles above Lee's Ferry. As water releases from the dam are dependent on power requirements that fluctuate daily, flows also fluctuate between 1,000 and 30,000 cubic feet per second. Sediment reaching Lake Powell, the artificial reservoir impounded behind the dam, settles out in the lake's quiet water. The water used in power generation comes from the clear depths of a reservoir, so the temperature of the river remains a chilly 45 to 55 degrees Fahrenheit. Lack of sediment may mean clear water for cooking and drinking, but unfortunately the sand and silt beaches eroded by the fluctuating river have a dramatically reduced source for replacement. Eventually there may be no sand beaches on which river runners can camp. In addition, the river's lower temperature and diurnal fluctuations have severely affected native fish populations.

At Mile 39.5, talus and other scars from test holes are visible on either bank. This is the proposed site for the Marble Canyon Dam. At one time, plans called for the construction of two dams in what is now Grand Canyon National Park. The first was to be built here, and its waters would have flooded 53 miles upstream. The second, Bridge Canyon Dam, Mile 236, would have flooded about 95 miles of river, including Lava Falls and the lower end of Havasu Canyon. As late as 1966, many expected that the dams would be built. But in June of that year, the Sierra Club paid for full-page advertisements in the New York *Times* and Washington *Post*. The duplicate advertisement, "Only You can Save the Grand Canyon from Being Flooded—For Profit," initiated a flood of protest aimed at stopping the dams. Public opposition resulted in a series of events intended to protect the rivers in Grand Canyon. In 1968, Congress passed Public Law 90-537 prohibiting the study or construction of hydroelectric dams in Grand Canyon without congressional approval. Finally, in 1975, President Ford signed the Grand Canyon Enlargement Act. As a result, Marble Canyon and the entire Grand Canyon to Grand Wash Cliffs became part of Grand Canyon National Park. It should be pointed out that the left bank, from Mile 165 to Mile 273, is still on the Hualapai Indian Reservation; and the inclusion of eastern Marble Canyon within the park, from the Paria to the Little Colorado River, is subject to approval of the Navajo Tribe.

In 1890, Stanton's second expedition discovered Peter Hansbrough's skeleton stretched out over the rocky shoreline above the rapid at Mile 43.7. Hansbrough, you may recall, had drowned at Mile 25.25 during the Stanton-Brown expedition six months earlier. On the morning of January 17, a demoralized crew buried Hansbrough beneath a "shaft of pure marble, seven hundred feet high," and named the promontory on the right bank "Point Hansbrough."

Mile 43.7
President
Harding Rapid
Map 5

A large boulder partially obstructs the river and forms a rapid near Hansbrough's grave. In 1923, the U.S. Geological Survey stopped to scout this noisy stretch. The expedition was the first to carry a radio receiver down the river. Several days earlier, at their Soap Creek camp, the party learned of President Harding's death. Later, as they pondered the "savage rapid" at mile 43, the crew elected to camp in observance of the president's funeral scheduled for the following day. Colonel Birdseye, leader of the expedition, called the stretch Boulder Rapid, although his subsequent map renamed the cataract President Harding Rapid.

In 1955, Bill Beer and John Daggett, the first men to swim Marble and Grand Canyon, experienced some excitement at President Harding Rapid. Beer, clinging to his waterproof neoprene pack, easily missed the huge rock. Daggett attempted to "fend himself off with his feet." After crashing into the Godzilla-sized boulder, Daggett emerged with deep cuts on his scalp and a badly scraped knuckle. Unperturbed, the two successfully completed their "run" through the Canyon.

Mile 52.3
Nankoweap Canyon
Map 5

Through driving frozen mist and whirling snow, a determined trail construction crew from U.S. Geological Survey reached the floor of "Nun-ko-weap" Valley in November 1882. After a day of rest, most of the crew, including the Survey's new director, John Wesley Powell, departed Nankoweap leaving a young geologist named Charles Walcott and three other men to explore and study the geology. For 72 days the crew labored, building horse trails over the high ridges which separated Nankoweap, Kwagunt, Chuar, and Unkar valleys. The work involved frequent risks, and Walcott often found himself on dangerous climbs. Once, while attempting to reach the Precambrian rocks south of Vishnu Temple, the party came to a narrow cleft: "In going out," wrote Walcott, "one mule was killed outright and two badly injured." Walcott's efforts eventually confirmed the Precambrian age for much of the area's rock formations, and ultimately he emerged as America's pioneer in the study of Precambrian life. Charles Walcott later served as Director of the U.S. Geological Survey from 1894 to 1907.

Nankoweap Canyon enters on the right as the main canyon assumes its characteristic asymmetrical profile. Here the river is one-half mile from the east rim and about seven from the west. Nankoweap Canyon contains scores of archaeological sites along its ten-mile course from the Kaibab Plateau to the Colorado River. Between A.D. 900 and 1150, prehistoric Pueblo people built most of the sites, including the cliff granaries observable from the river.

The Pueblo lifeway began in the southern Colorado Plateau, a vast area dissected by the drainages of the Colorado, Little Colorado, and San Juan rivers. The ancestral Pueblo, the Basketmakers, evolved from the ancient Desert Culture about the time of Christ. As their name implies, these people created exceptionally fine baskets. They also practiced agriculture, supplementing their economy with corn and squash.

By A.D. 800, as they began to construct aboveground masonry houses and improve their pottery. Basketmaker Culture evolved into a lifeway archaeologists call Pueblo. By the middle of the eleventh century, the classic Pueblo had developed in the distinct population centers of Mesa Verde, Chaco Canyon, and Kayenta. During this period the Pueblo people constructed the grand multi-storied cliff dwelling at Mesa Verde and the massive 800-room Pueblo Bonita at Chaco Canyon.

Beginning about A.D. 700, a few Kayenta people began seasonal occupation of the depths of the Grand Canyon. By 1000, their population grew until hundreds of people inhabited the Grand Canyon region. Of the 2,700 canyon sites known, possibly 1,500 were utilized between 1050 and 1150. According to archaeological evidence, Nankoweap contained no permanent residents prior to A.D. 1000, although hunters from the rim occasionally pursued game into the canyon at least 10,000 years ago. The first settlers probably occupied the upper drainage to take advantage of greater moisture or to remain close to the rim's familiar environment. The first residents undoubtedly encountered a variety of problems in their new environment. The unvegetated inner canyon, as opposed to the forested rim, made the pursuit of game more difficult. In addition, women needed to learn the life cycles of new plants, and wood for construction and fire was scarce. In spite of these difficulties, by 1050, more families descended into Nankoweap, possibly because of diminishing farmland above or pressure from nomadic people. Some people remained near the earlier families closest to the rim. Others dwelt in the middle valley. A few reached the delta of the Colorado

River where they continued to farm, hunt, and gather. Pueblo people migrated out of Nankoweap and the rest of the Grand Canyon about 1200-1225. Much drier climatic conditions and a reduction of arable lands due to erosion, particularly arroyo or gully cutting, may have prompted the exodus.

Mile 56.6
Kwagunt
Canyon
Map 6

Kwagunt, a Southern Paiute, lived in or near the canyon that now bears his name. According to linguistic and archaeological evidences, Kwagunt's Paiute ancestors spread southwestward from the Great Basin into the desert Southwest sometime after A.D. 1000. The Southern Paiute continued the simple hunting and gathering lifestyle of the Desert Archaic, a culture that began about 9000 B.C. An extensive knowledge of their environment allowed the Paiute to utilize a variety of food resources. Their diet included, among other things, deer, mice, snakes, lizards, and wild plants, as well as cultivated corn, squash, beans, and potatoes. Although their diet would not always appeal to our more fastidious tastes, the Paiute survived in an environment that often starved white explorers.

Paiute men

In the late 1700s, Southern Paiutes occupied southern Utah, northern Arizona, and the deserts of southern Nevada and California. By the end of the first decade of the twentieth century, all semblance of native Southern Paiute life had vanished. Today, the Southern Paiute have five small reservations: Kaibab north of the Grand Canyon, Shivwits near St. George, Utah, Willow Springs, Arizona, and Moapa and Las Vegas in southern Nevada.

From the east, 3,000 feet beneath Cape Solitude, the Little Colorado River enters the main gorge. This large tributary drains about 26,900 square miles of Arizona and New Mexico. After a storm, the Little Colorado sometimes flows a thick, muddy brown with a volume greater than the Colorado mainstream. The stream often flows a rich, milky blue at a near constant discharge of about 200 cubic feet per second. The largest source, Blue Springs,

Mile 61.5
Little Colorado River
Map 6

gushes from the Redwall about 12.5 miles upstream. The Little Colorado, laden with salt, calcium carbonate, and alkaline earth metals, is not recommended for drinking if other sources are available. The river, however, provides an extremely important reproductive habitat for a near-extinct species of fish once common in the Colorado River drainage: the humpback chub, one of the four remaining native species of fish surviving in the Grand Canyon. For this reason, fishing or bathing with soap or shampoo is not permitted in the tributary.

The Little Colorado's high salt content, coupled with the frequency and severity of floods, undoubtedly discouraged prehistoric farmers from occupying the narrow gorge. Nevertheless, the Hopi, and possibly their Pueblo ancestors, considered the junction of the Little Colorado and the main stream sacred. Salt located in deposits near Mile 63 on the Colorado is used by the Hopi for ceremonial purposes. The ancient trail to these sanctified deposits begins in Moenkopi and enters the Little Colorado seven miles up the tributary at Salt Trail Canyon. A few miles downstream this route passes a spring situated on top of a forty-foot orange travertine dome. According to Hopi belief, this is the original Sipapu, or Sipapuni, from which mankind emerged.

In 1869, Powell located a Pueblo ruin and fragments of pottery near the mouth of the Little Colorado. The original structure no longer exists. A prospector named Ben Beamer arrived at the confluence between 1880 and 1882 and probably used material from the ruin to construct a stone cabin a few hundred yards up the Little Colorado. Analysis of the Beamer site indicates visitation by twelfth-century Pueblo, Southern Paiute, Pai, and Hopi people long before Beamer remodeled the dwelling in 1890. (As is the case with all historical sites, visitors are asked to protect the ruin and not disturb any artifact.)

*Confluence of
Colorado and Little
Colorado Rivers
from Cape Solitude*

In 1869, Powell's desperate crew spent three days
at the Little Colorado before continuing their journey
into the "Great Unknown." For reasons not entirely
clear, Powell considered the Little Colorado as the
division between Marble Canyon and Grand Canyon.
Although Powell did not name the Grand Canyon,
his exploits and writings popularized the name and
insured its acceptance. Powell, apprehensive of what
lay below the Little Colorado, wrote: "We have an
unknown distance to run, an unknown river to
explore. What falls there are, we know not: what
rocks beset the channel, we know not. Ah, well! we
may conjecture many things. The men talk as cheer-
fully as ever: jests are bandied about freely this morn-

ing; but to me the cheer is somber and the jests are ghastly."

Mile 65.6
Lava Canyon
Map 7

On the right bank, immediately above Lava Canyon Rapid, an abandoned adit overlooks the river. The mine is probably the Copper Grant, operated by George McCormick around 1904. About 1880 to 1907, McCormick also operated the "Tanner" mine across the river near the mouth of Palisades Creek. Seth B. Tanner, a Mormon settler from Tuba City, prospected in the area during the 1880s. Tanner Trail, Tanner Canyon, and Tanner Rapid all bear Seth's name.

Mile 71.0
Cardenas Creek
Map 7

In September 1540, after twenty days of rough travel from the Hopi villages in the east, an entourage of Spanish explorers arrived at the South Rim, possibly in the vicinity of Desert View. The leader of this group, the first non-Indians to examine the canyon, was García López Cárdenas, a competent and tough lieutenant of explorer Francisco Vasquez de Coronado. The Spaniards, unaccustomed to Grand Canyon perspectives, grossly underestimated the canyon's depth and breadth and assumed the river to be about six feet wide. Their Hopi guides assured the explorers that the river was much wider but offered no information on how to reach the bottom. After three days of futile effort to locate the descending route, Cárdenas directed Captain Pablo de Melgosa, Juan Galeras, and one other man to scramble as best they could down into the giant chasm. Unable to descend more than one-third of the canyon's depth, the men returned late that afternoon convinced of the magnitude of the Grand Canyon. Low on water and patience, Cárdenas returned to Coronado's main party at Zuni. For the next 200 years no white man is known to have entered the canyon.

The extensive Unkar delta contains the largest known prehistoric settlement along the river in Grand Canyon. Archaeological excavations conducted in 1967 and 1968 revealed evidence of Pueblo occupations beginning about A.D. 950 and ending about 1150. The earliest inhabitants consisted of a few families who built a multi-roomed structure on the low ledge overlooking upper Unkar Rapid, as well as other structures. Architectural and ceramic evidence indicates a rather short period of occupation, after which the Unkar delta remained abandoned for about 100 years. About 1080, another Pueblo group settled at Unkar and practiced agriculture. Within a decade they constructed three large multi-roomed dwellings, two smaller dwellings, and a large circular subterranean structure. Before 1150 the number of structures increased to include many small multi-room sites, well-developed agricultural terraces, and other sites. The settlement, however, endured only briefly. The drier climatic conditions and accelerated erosion that apparently forced the abandonment of the rest of the canyon probably affected the Unkar people as well. By 1200, no Pueblo dwelt in the Grand Canyon.

Mile 72.5
Unkar Rapid
Map 7

Norman D. Nevills entered the river-running business by accepting $50 to lead a San Juan River trip. Before his party of three prepaid guests arrived, he hurriedly constructed a boat out of lumber scrounged from a nearby barn and outhouse. By 1938, Nevills had gained sufficient confidence to offer the first commercial boat trip through the Grand Canyon. His pioneer guests included the first women to complete the voyage: Elzada Clover, a botany instructor, and Lois Jotter, a student. Using his plywood cataract boats, Nevills conducted seven Grand Canyon transits.

Mile 75.5
Nevills Rapid
Map 7

✕

Norman Nevills,
1949

Mile 76.5
Hance Rapid
Map 8

Red Canyon, undoubtedly named for the brilliant Hakatai redbeds through which it cuts, enters on the left. Debris washed down the canyon creates an imposing pile of rocks and rumbling water named Hance Rapid, after "Captain" John Hance, Grand Canyon's first permanent settler. Hance constructed the first rim hotel and cultivated a reputation for outlandish storytelling. For example, Hance often recounted a snowshoe trek over the dense clouds that filled the canyon. Midway through this ethereal journey, a clearing trend nearly cost John his life as he scrambled across a disintegrating cloud field for the safety of a nearby pinnacle. In another story, John was pursued by hostile Indians. Upon reaching the rim, he convinced his skeptical pony "Old Dusty" to attempt to jump the Canyon. Less than halfway across they realized they would not make it. Reluctantly, they turned around in mid-flight and returned to face the Indians. Hance survived the encounter. He also constructed the Old Hance and Red Canyon trails from the South Rim to the river. The asbestos mine downstream at Asbestos Canyon is another Hance project.

On October 21, 1896, George F. Flavell and Ramon Montos boated to the head of Hance Rapid. Like most

John Hance

of the early river runners, George and Ramon were inclined to portage the rock-studded stretch. As they surveyed the river, the river men were surprised by three horsemen from the South Rim who approached the river and dismounted. Flavell recounted his adventure to his interested guests. With an impressed audience at the sidelines, the macho crew reversed their decision to portage and prepared for the first confirmed run of Hance Rapid. In order to safely negotiate the left channel, the crew "had to make exact points," wrote Flavell, "which we failed to do." In seconds the river destroyed an oar and oarlock as the swift current trapped their wooden craft *Panthon* against the boulders. Flavell and Montos removed their pants and shoes and crawled out of their stricken boat. With their recently broken oar, the two men managed to pry the *Panthon* free. The boat and humbled crew crashed through the remaining distance as the spectators looked on. After a few repairs, the *Panthon* and her intrepid crew completed their adventure, running all the rapids in Marble and Grand canyons except Soap Creek. This was the third successful downriver run.

Mile 77.4
Upper Granite Gorge
Map 8

When the fast water below Hance Rapid subsides and the boats float peacefully in quiet water, the visitor may notice a somber change in the canyon walls. Black, hard rocks replace the colorful shales of the Grand Canyon Supergroup as the river enters the realm of the Vishnu Schist, some of the oldest rocks exposed on the continent. These ancient rocks consist primarily of mica schists originally deposited as muds and sands along lowlands and shallow coastal waters over two billion years ago. About 1.7 billion years ago the earth's internal forces uplifted the region into an extensive mountain range. Extreme pressures and temperatures altered the old shales into an entirely different metamorphosed rock called schist. About 1.5 to 1.6 billion years ago, lightcolored molten granite intruded into the darker schists. The abundance of granitic outcrops within the schist, and the fact that the hard Vishnu creates its own rapid-filled inner chasm, prompted early explorers to call this region the Granite Gorge. There are three similar gorges within the Grand Canyon. The next 40 miles of river is referred to as the First or Upper Granite Gorge.

On August 14, 1869, the Powell expedition arrived above a rapid where "the rushing waters break into great waves on the rocks, and lash themselves into a mad, white foam." Convinced that a portage was impossible, the party of nine decided to run the rapid. "The waves were frightful beyond anything we have yet met and it seemed for a time that our chance to save the boats was very slim but we are a lusty set and our good luck did not go back on us then," wrote crewman George Bradley. Three years later Powell's second expedition ran the "Gate of Hell" cataract and named it Sockdolager, a slang term meaning a heavy or knockdown blow.

Mile 78.5
Sockdolager Rapid
Map 8

If Sockdolager offered a thrill to both Powell expeditions, Grapevine Rapid provided only misery. Midway through a difficult lining attempt, the first expedition spent a gloomy, rain-filled night huddled among the boulders on the right bank. Three years later, the second expedition, drenched by bone-chilling rain as a rapidly rising river battered their wooden boats against the dark schist, endured two dreadful nights as they lined the steep-walled rapid.

Mile 81.5
Grapevine Rapid
Map 8

In July 1960, "Fireball" Young powered the 18-foot jet boat *Wee Yellow* upstream into Grapevine Rapid. Young was part of a four-boat, nine-man upriver run from Lake Mead to Lee's Ferry. Midway up the rapid a huge hole stood the fiberglass boat on its nose as a fountain-like plume from the waterjet filled the air. "With a roar and a final sputter," *Wee Yellow* vanished beneath the turbulent tailwaves of Grapevine. In spite of the mishap the three remaining jet boats soon reached Lee's Ferry in the first and only successful upriver run through the Grand Canyon.

Mile 87.7
Bright Angel Creek
Map 9

After a miserable night at Grapevine Rapid, the starving 1869 Powell party arrived at the mouth of a lovely, clear stream they named Silver Creek. Later, Powell renamed the stream Bright Angel. The crew devoted the next two days to repairing boats and sawing oars from a pine brought down the creek by an earlier flood. The crew, struggling along with their remaining ten days' worth of musty flour, a few dried apples, and "plenty of coffee," must endure another 200 miles of raging river.

Phantom Ranch lies a quarter-mile up Bright Angel Creek. The "ranch," actually a cluster of small wood and stone cabins, a dining hall, and dormitories, was constructed in 1922 as an overnight tourist stop by park concessioner Fred Harvey. Phantom Ranch is called Rust's Camp on an earlier tourist camp, named after David Rust, an early Grand Canyon guide. The black Kaibab Bridge crossing the Colorado upstream of Bright Angel Creek was built in 1928 to replace an

Dave Rust's camp on Bright Angel Creek, 1907-08; now Phantom Ranch

older swinging bridge. Downstream, the 522-foot aluminum bridge is part of a water pipeline project begun in 1965. The pipeline brings water from Roaring Springs below the North Rim to the South Rim.

In low water, Horn Creek Rapid, a splashy, bubbling, hideous place, is worthy of any profanity thrown its way during a century of river running. Powell preferred to line Horn and in doing so damaged the *Canyon Maid*. After lining one boat in 1890, Robert Stanton attempted what he called the "Powell plan" of rapid transit: "turn the boat loose at the head of the rapid and catch them below." This innovative method reduced the *Marie* to a floating mat of kindling. Stanton's remaining boat was cautiously lined around Horn Creek Rapid.

Mile 90.5
Horn Creek Rapid
Map 9

On February 20, 1929, Glen E. Sturdevant, chief naturalist of Grand Canyon National Park, and two other men attempted a boat crossing above Horn. After losing an oar, the unfortunate crew was swept into the rapid where Sturdevant and Fred Johnson drowned. The third man, James Brooks, reached the shore safely.

Louis Boucher, a silent man and "typical prospector, possessing geology pick, pan, and tools for trail making," built the trail that descends from the rim to Boucher Canyon. Boucher's quiet nature and isolated lifestyle earned him the title "the hermit." Near his copper mine at Long (Boucher) Canyon, Louis planted an orchard and garden where he grew oranges, pomegranates, and a variety of other fruits and vegetables. His mining attempts apparently proved unproductive, because by 1912 he had moved to a small Utah town. Hermit Canyon, Hermit Rapid, the Hermit Trail, Boucher Canyon, and Boucher Rapid are named after this reticent prospector.

Mile 94.9
Hermit Rapid
Map 9

Hermit Camp near
Hermit Creek,
1912-30

In January 1908, Edward Monett and Charles Russell attempted to line Hermit Rapid. The powerful current soon relieved them of their boat, the *Utah*, and the two luckless adventurers were obliged to start walking. The novelty of minor disaster wore thin for Monett and Russell. Their long-planned river trip had scarcely begun when a third crewman, Bert Loper, damaged his boat and camera in Cataract Canyon, 200 miles above Lee's Ferry. To help finance the trip, Bert expected to sell photographs of the journey. After the mishap, he sent the camera out for repairs once they reached the river crossing at Hite, Utah. Loper agreed to meet the others at Lee's Ferry on December 1, one month away. The camera arrived November 20th, but Loper waited thirty-two days to depart. Monett and Russell, undoubtedly perplexed by Loper's tardiness, departed Lee's Ferry on December 13, two weeks after the agreed date. As Bert peacefully procrastinated in a quiet section of Glen Canyon, Russell frantically rescued Monett from his boat, which was hopelessly lodged between boulders in the midst of a rapid upstream of Bright Angel. Reduced to one boat, Monett had little choice but to cling in abalone fashion to the stern deck of Russell's craft as they continued downriver. After their Hermit lining fiasco, the two men stumbled across Boucher and spent the night at his cabin. Louis suggested that the lost *Utah* might be in the eddy at Boucher Rapid. The two river men hiked down to the location and found that the hermit had guessed right. After a few repairs, Monett and Russell resumed their journey and arrived at Needles, California, one month later.

Believing the stream to be Shinumo Creek, Robert Stanton stopped at Crystal Creek on February 8, 1890, to climb Point Sublime. Here a disgruntled crewman, Harry McDonald, elected to abandon the expedition. After an arduous winter trek, Harry arrived "nearer dead than alive" at a line shack on Buckskin Mountain (Kaibab Plateau).

Mile 98.0
Crystal Creek
Map 10

Before 1966, the mild rapid at Crystal appeared "much like Boucher, long, wide and slow at first, steep and clear at the last." The rapid is scarcely mentioned in any early river accounts, although the Carnegie Institute expedition portaged the upper section in November 1937. An unusually intense storm began on December 7, 1966, and dumped fourteen inches of rain in a thirty-six hour period along the North Rim. The resulting flood in Crystal's upper drainages obliterated Pueblo sites that had escaped floods for the previous 900 years. Crystal Creek's rampaging water and mud flows pushed the debris fan 200 feet farther into the Colorado, creating an impressive, ulcer-generating spectacle called Crystal Rapid.

Mile 99.5
Willie's Necktie
Map 10

In spite of his advanced age and heart condition, Wilson B. Taylor enjoyed running the Colorado. His trips included the 1948 Ed Hudson upriver attempt, Willie's first Grand Canyon downriver trip in 1949, and the motorboat traverse of 1950 with Bill Belknap, river historian Otis "Dock" Marston, and others. During the 1950 adventure, a powerful current pinned the hard-hulled, 125-horsepower *Esmeralda II* against the right wall at lower Tuna Rapid. When Willie fell out, rescuers tossed him a line, which unfortunately wrapped "a turn or two" around the elderly gentleman's neck. Without the care normally

Wilson Taylor (second from Left) and Esmeralda II

reserved for a man of Wilson's age, crewmen hauled him back to safety. Willie survived the ordeal and the rapid was christened "Willie's Necktie." Six years later, Willie died of a heart attack in Marble Canyon. He was buried near the river at Mile 44.5.

William Wallace Bass, a prospector, miner, and tour guide, arrived at the Grand Canyon about 1884. Bass constructed a trail from his South Rim tourist camp to the river and up Shinumo Canyon, where he developed a tent camp, garden, and orchard. Early river crossings required a boat, but by 1908 Bass had installed a cable crossing with a cage large enough for horses. (In 1968, the Park Service cut the cable, located at Mile 108, but remnants of it and the cage are still visible on the left bank, twenty feet above the river.) Bass' tourist operation grossed up to $21,000 a year. By 1920, over 3,000 people had registered at Bass' South Rim camp, which he and his family continued to operate until 1923. Bass, 84, died in 1933. As he wished, his ashes were scattered over Holy Grail Temple.

Mile 107.8
Bass Rapid
Map 11

In 1916, Charles Russell began his second Colorado River adventure. Abandoned by fellow adventurers, and having lost two boats along the way, Russell, August Tadje, and a Mr. Clements bravely departed Bright Angel in the spring of 1915 to continue their epic cinematographic expeditions. All went well until Crystal Rapid. Afterwards, the trio continued downstream in their remaining boat, the *Ross Wheeler*. Behind them, along the river's bottom, bounced their second boat, all their film, and a camera. The *Ross Wheeler* is parked in the rocks above Bass Rapid, abandoned by the weary crew.

Above Hakatai Rapid, on the left bank, are the remains of a cable crossing built by William Bass sometime after 1908 to provide access to his asbestos mine up Hakatai Canyon. "Hakatai" is the Havasupai word for the Colorado River.

Mile 110.9
Hakatai Rapid
Map 11

*River crossing at
Bass Trail*

Mile 112.1
**Waltenberg
Rapid**
Map 11

Little is known about John Waltenberg, helper and occasional partner of William Bass for about eighteen years. John came from Wisconsin and, according to Bass, could be located anywhere in the canyon by following his trail of tobacco spit. No ladies' man, Waltenberg avoided women and apparently never spoke about them. In 1917, he spent over a month helping Levi Noble map the Shinumo Quadrangle. John ultimately found work in Noble's southern California orange grove.

In December 1911, Emery and Ellsworth Kolb forsook the South Rim's sub-zero weather and, at Bright Angel, resumed their photographic expedition.

The brothers were joined by a new crew member, Bert Lauzon, a miner and cowboy. On December 24, this intrepid, shivering party arrived at Waltenberg Rapid. Ellsworth selected a "channel" down the left, while Emery preferred the "least dangerous" right hand run. Bert walked. A moment after Emery's *Edith* parked midstream in a pile of rocks, Ellsworth's *Defiance* upset in the icy river. Sensing the urgency of the moment, Emery gallantly pried the *Edith* free and promptly smashed her on the boulders below. In the meantime, Ellsworth painfully crawled out of the river and watched his clothing freeze. Bert swam out and retrieved the wayward *Defiance*. These frosty voyagers spent the following day, December 25, thawing out and repairing the *Edith* somewhere below Waltenberg, or "Christmas," Rapid.

John Waltenberg

Mile 126.0
Middle Granite
Gorge
Map 12

The contact of Tapeats sandstone with the dark schist near 127 Mile Rapid marks the beginning of the second, and shortest, of the Grand Canyon's three Granite gorges. The Middle Granite Gorge ends four miles downstream, immediately below Bedrock Rapid.

Mile 130.4
"Dreadrock"
Rapid
Map 12

At the bottom of the Middle Granite Gorge awaits a small rapid with a very big rock in the center. Here the river's main flow strikes a restaurant-sized boulder and deflects left. The right-hand route offers considerably fewer thrills and is usually the preferred run.

On a hot summer's day, 1973, a silver 37-foot pontoon motored toward Bedrock Rapid. The lead boatman, weary from a long day of rapids, relinquished control of his fourteen-passenger craft to his enthusiastic though inexperienced apprentice boatman. In later years, that raw recruit became one of the canyon's most competent guides; at that distant moment above Bedrock, however, Myron Cook's career languished as he roared toward Bedrock's left-hand run. The lead boatman glanced up and screamed, "Go right!" Unfortunately, too little time remained to actually do that. The sleek craft, with its full complement of previously pampered passengers, was pushed broadside against the huge rock. Moments later the powerful current caught the upstream sidetube and rolled the great boat over. No one was hurt, although most of the sleeping gear and food washed downstream. The boat remained intact, and as the humbled-yet-wiser boatman recalled, "About every soul on that river came to the rescue." Passing boat parties helped right the pontoon and provided enough food for Cook's grateful adventurers to complete their trip.

River running for the early adventurers often proved toilsome. Many of the rapids were viewed as obstacles that required lining or a portage. Heavy, round-bottomed, and easily upset, the early unmaneuverable boats were not designed for whitewater. Fastwater and flatwater rowing techniques remained identical: in order to steer, the boat was rowed fast enough to make use of a tiller-like sweep oar. This simple style proved splendid for chasing whales on the open ocean, but when applied in whitewater it produced the results described by Frederick Dellenbaugh in 1872:

Mile 131.5
Galloway
Canyon
Map 12

> I pulled the bow oars, and my back was toward the terrific roar which, like the voice of some awful monster, grew louder as we approached. It was difficult to refrain from turning around to see what it looked like now, but as everything depended on the promptness with which Hillers and I handled our oars in obedience to Powell's orders, I waited for the plunge, every instant ready to execute a command. . . . Then of a sudden there was a dropping away of all support, a reeling sensation, and we flew down the declivity with the speed of a locomotive. The gorge was in chaos. The boat rolled and plunged. The wild waters rolled over us, filling the open spaces to the gunwale.

This technique, thrilling as it was, afforded the crew little opportunity to control the boat once they entered a rapid. There had to be a better way.

In 1891, a Utah trapper and prospector, Nathaniel Galloway, began running rivers. Galloway concluded that a light-weight, maneuverable boat capable of missing obstructions proved superior to earlier types. Most importantly, Galloway decided to face downstream as he rowed, avoiding the hazards as he saw them. This rowing technique is used in whitewater today. In 1897, Galloway and William C. Richmond boated the canyon in their 16-foot 30-inch-wide wooden boats. Later, as head boatman for the 1909 Julius Stone expedition, Galloway became the first person to boat the entire Grand Canyon twice. The side canyon near Mile 131.6 is named after this important river runner.

Mile 131.8
**Dubendorff
Rapid**
Map 12

Galloway Canyon and Stone Creek, the latter canyon named after industrialist-explorer Julius Stone, create a surprisingly vigorous rapid. In 1909, Galloway attempted a run and soon found himself anchored upon the rocks on the right. Stone decided to run left and successfully negotiated the rapid. Seymour Dubendorff followed Stone's example with one notable exception: he capsized in a large wave at the top. The rapid now bears Dubendorff's name.

*Dubendorff Rapid,
1949*

In July 1927, the Clyde Eddy expedition endured its share of grief at Dubendorff. Partway through a lining attempt, swift water pinned the *Powell* broadside against the rocks. After four days of fruitless labor, the crew gave up their salvage attempt and continued downstream in their two remaining boats.

During the 1940 Norman Nevills expedition, Doris Nevills, Norm's wife, washed overboard at the unnamed rapid one mile below Deercreek. Subsequent Nevills river runners and others began calling the rapid "Doris."

Mile 137.7
Doris Rapid
Map 13

Located over a mile above Fishtail, Doris Rapid is surprisingly active during high water. In July 1960, the *Wee Yellow*, one of the four jetboats on the Hamilton upriver run, took on about sixty gallons of water here and, with her engine sputtering, beached below. Remembering their two-day struggle to climb Vulcan Rapid (Lava Falls), the crew christened the rapid Little Vulcan. A few days later *Wee Yellow* sank in Grapevine Rapid.

Kanab, a Paiute word for "willows," has its headwaters in Utah's Pausagunt Plateau, 100 miles to the north. In September 1872, Powell's second expedition stopped at Kanab Creek for supplies brought down by pack train from the town of Kanab, Utah, about 50 miles up the canyon. Troubled by the Colorado's rising flood waters and reports of Indian hostilities, Powell allowed his crew two days' rest before announcing, "Well, boys, our voyage is done!" The crew's response ranged from disappointment to barely concealed glee. Powell's earlier river expedition and subsequent land explorations near Toroweap, in addition to Wheeler's strange 1871 upriver expedition to Diamond Creek, apparently satiated the Major's lust for knowledge. "We were in the field to accomplish certain work and not to perform a

Mile 143.5
Kanab Creek
Map 14

spectacular feat," wrote crewman Dellenbaugh. Still, one wonders: did the Major chicken out at Kanab?

Mile 150.0
Upset Rapid
Map 14

In September 1923, the U.S. Geological Survey expedition arrived at the unnamed rapid at 150 Mile Canyon. Head boatman Emery Kolb rowed his boat *Marble* into the huge hole at the bottom and flipped. Uninjured, Kolb climbed on the derelict craft's bottom, leaving behind a rapid with its new name—Upset.

In June 1967, Jesse "Shorty" Burton, a professional boatman, capsized his motorized pontoon at Upset and drowned. Shorty's lifejacket apparently caught on the motor mount. His epitaph is scratched on the small metal plate wired to a rock below the rapid.

Mile 156.8
Havasu Creek
Map 15

Havasu Creek enters from the south immediately above a small rapid near Mile 157. The stream's rich, blue-green waters rise from perennial springs well over ten miles up Havasu, or Cataract, Canyon. Five spectacular waterfalls account for a third of the 1,400-foot drop in elevation from the springs to the Colorado River.

Upper Havasu is the traditional summer home of the Havasupai, the "People of the Blue-green Waters." Their recently enlarged reservation begins at Beaver Falls, about four and one-half miles from the river. Supai, the Havasupai village, lies about six miles beyond Beaver. Traditionally, the Havasupai followed an annual cycle of plateau and canyon occupation. In the early spring they descended into the canyon as the plateau snows disappeared and a water source was needed. By mid-April, planting began at Supai. Diverted water from Havasu Creek allowed the cultivation of crops, including corn, beans, sunflowers, melons, peaches, and apricots. During the winter months, most of the Havasupai wandered

Mooney Falls,
Havasu Canyon

up to the plateau to hunt and gather wild plants and seeds. For six months the Havasupai pursued a hunting and gathering subsistence pattern similar to their Paiute and Hualapai neighbors. On the plateaus they gathered piñon nuts, agave, and other plants. They also hunted a variety of game animals, including deer, rabbits and an occasional antelope.

Fray Francisco Garces, probably the first European to actually visit Havasu Canyon, arrived at a village he called "Jabesúa" in June 1776. Garces remained in the village five days and then returned to Hopi. By

Havasupai woman,
late 19th century

1880 visits by Anglo-American miners and prospective homesteaders had increased, causing concern among the Havasupai, as well as to the Commissioner of Indian Affairs. In 1882, President Chester Arthur approved a 518-acre reservation consisting of bottom land surrounding the Supai, totally ignoring the Havasupai's dependence upon the plateau. The 1975 Grand Canyon Enlargement act expanded the traditional use area within the Park, and the reservation was enlarged to 185,000 acres.

Mile 164.0
The Hualapai
People
Map 15

The Hualapai Reservation begins on the left bank a short distance below Tuckup Canyon. Their land extends to Mile 273. The Hualapai, culturally and linguistically only slightly different from the Havasupai, call themselves Ja Whala Pa'a, the "Pine Tree Mountain People." Like other Yuman-speaking people, the Hualapai (sometimes spelled Walapai) believed they descended from people created from reeds of the Colorado River. In the beginning, the Creator, Matavila, lived alone at the sacred cave, Whaḥávo, overlooking the copious spring of Mata Widita Canyon. It was Matavila who cut the canes and prayed to give them life, creating the various tribes along the lower Colorado River.

Archaeological evidence indicates that the Hualapai and Havasupai, collectively referred to as the Northeastern Pai, occupied northwestern central Arizona for over a millennium. The Northeastern Pai's hunting and gathering culture allowed them to survive the great droughts of the twelfth and thirteenth centuries that drove the Anasazi Pueblo people to the permanent villages of the Hopi mesas and the Rio Grande valley.

Although the Pai relied upon the seasonal exploitation of wild plants and game, they did practice agriculture to a certain extent. The most extensive agricultural effort occurred in Havasu Canyon. The Pai also diverted water for crops along Diamond Creek and at Indian Gardens. Permanent springs at Peach Springs, Mata Widita, and Quartermaster canyons provided water for garden plots. Their principal crop was pumpkin, although squash, maize, and beans were also cultivated. The Pai collected wild plants, including the rich, oily seeds of sélé or mentzelia, the sweet fruit of the prickly pear cactus, piñon, and a variety of other plants. When food stores ran low in the spring and early summer, hungry Pai resorted to viyal, the century plant. With the sharp end of a long stick, the Pai would sever the plant at its base. Afterward, they trimmed the leaves with a stone blade and stacked the viyal hearts in a pit lined with pre-heated rocks. Green leaves and a layer of dirt covered the oven. After one or two days of slow roasting, the sweet and tart viyal hearts were removed and usually dried in the sun for later consumption or trade.

Like the Great Basin gatherers, the Pai were not known for their exquisite shelters. Usually rock shelters or branches propped against a tree sufficed for home. If the Pai's mode of life allowed little time for elaborate dwelling construction, it allowed even less for illness. Sick Pai usually recovered quickly or died. Survivors quickly cremated the dead, so the kwidjati, the soul, would not linger to haunt the living. Friends, not close relatives, would handle the corpse. Afterward, they would burn their clothes and thoroughly wash themselves in yucca soap.

Like most native populations, the Hualapai suffered greatly at the hands of the whites. The murder of a Pai leader in 1866 initiated a series of hostilities referred to as the Walapai War. By 1869, the war ended and the Hualapai were removed to the Colorado River Indian Reservation at La Paz, Arizona. After a long year of disease and frustration, 600 Hualapais left La Paz and scattered throughout their original homeland. In 1883, the U.S. government created a reservation that eventually contained 997,045 acres. Today, the 900-member tribe supports itself through livestock production and tourism.

Mile 179.0
Lava Falls
Map 17

On August 25, 1869, Powell's expedition arrived at "a fall, or the nearest approach to it of any on the river," and called the rapid Lava Falls. Several crewmen postulated that the falls are the remnant of the mammoth lava dams that once impounded the Colorado. Powell attributed the rapids' origin to the "boulders some distance below the ancient dams." Lava Falls, like all major rapids in the Grand Canyon, is the result of erosional debris discharged into the main river from a tributary canyon, in this case, Prospect Canyon.

In September 1867, a pathetic figure clinging desperately to a makeshift log raft may have been the first person to "run" all the rapids of Grand Canyon, Lava Falls included. Two years before Powell's celebrated river exploration, three men pulled a starving, raving, severely sunburned remnant of a human being from the river near Calville, Nevada. The hapless body belonged to James White, a prospector who, after a brief convalescence, told an amazing tale of Indian attacks, treacherous rapids, hunger, and relentless sun. Surely, his rescuers thought, White's incredible journey carried him through the uncharted Grand Canyon. Soon numerous, if embellished, accounts of White's exploits appeared in text and newspaper. The legend soon emerged as the focal point of an often bitter, sometimes silly controversy.

White's adventure began in western Colorado. After stealing horses "from Indians" and wounding a partner in a gunfight, White, along with Charles Baker and George Strole, started prospecting in the San Juan drainage. Indians killed Baker and forced the two survivors to a river where they hastily constructed a driftwood raft. Strole perished in a rapid. White, after a two-week, true wilderness experience, emerged starving and half-baked at Calville. The site now lies beneath Lake Mead. To this day, no one knows if White actually made the trip through the Grand Canyon.

Lava Falls, celebrated in poem, prose, prayer, and frequent profanity, has caught the attention of river runners since White's days. Powell and Stanton, leaders of the first two river expeditions to see Lava, decided to portage its bubbling reaches. The first confirmed run was made by George Flavell in 1896. Flavell, departing from his usual theatrical style, wrote, "A bad rapid was run which put about 8 inches of water in the boat." Old George was getting used to the river.

In spite of George's success, most of the early expeditions continued to portage Lava on the left. After lining the rapid, the 1923 U.S. Geological Survey expedition camped on the left bank immediately below the falls. That evening the river began a twenty-one-foot rise as the flow increased from 10,000 to over 100,000 cubic feet per second by the following afternoon. Most of the rise was attributed to flooding in the Little Colorado drainage. The confused party devoted most of the sleepless night to protecting the boats from the rapidly rising river. At one time they were forced to row downstream in an "eerie night ride" amidst an inky-black, surging current to a camp probably near the bottom spring above the cliff at lower Lava. In the morning the crew found themselves in the middle of what was once the short rapid they lined the day before. Lava Falls "now stretched downstream as far as the eye could see, a tumble of racing water with some of the big waves running fully 20-feet high and throwing spray much higher." The water subsided four days later, allowing the expedition to continue its historic voyage.

Mile 198.5
Parashont
Wash
Map 18

In June 1946, after what must have been a grueling 80-mile hike from St. George, Utah, Harry Aleson and Georgie White arrived at the mouth of Parashont Wash. They inflated their one-man raft and floated down to Lake Mead. Two years earlier, this intrepid duo had jumped in the river at Diamond Creek and, wearing bathing suits, lifejackets, and tennis shoes, floated on 65,000 cubic feet per second of river to the lake. Harry was a well-known river guide and Georgie White, later Georgie Clark, became the first and undoubtedly the most famous woman river outfitter.

Mile 205.4
Kolb Rapid
Map 19

Emery Clifford Kolb arrived at the South Rim in 1902. He and his brother, Ellsworth, eventually opened a photographic studio, taking photos of tourists riding the canyon mules and later selling the pictures to the excited dudes. The Kolb brothers are best known for their river exploits. Their 1911-12 Colorado River expedition was the first Grand Can-

yon boat trip recorded on motion-picture film. Emery served as chief boatman for the 1923 U.S. Geological Survey expedition. Ellsworth moved to California in 1924, leaving Emery the South Rim studio. In 1974, Ron Smith's Grand Canyon expedition escorted Emery Kolb, 94, on his last river trip through a portion of the canyon. Emery, resident of the Grand Canyon for over seventy years, died on December 11, 1976. Shortly afterward, the Western River Guides Association, an organization of professional guides, requested that 205 Mile Rapid be renamed Kolb Rapid.

Mile 215.0
Lower Gorge
Map 20

Below Three Springs Canyon, the river carves into the igneous and metamorphic rocks of the lower Granite Gorge. In 1869, Powell's desperate party, remembering the violent rapids of the Upper Gorge, approached the dreaded formation. "It is with no little misgivings that we see the river enter these black, hard walls," wrote Powell. Physically exhausted, their morale low, the men prepare to battle a river that refused to end.

Mile 217.5
217 Mile Rapid
Map 20

Powell's expedition portaged 217 Mile Rapid, the first major rapid of the Lower Gorge. In June 1948, the cataract thwarted Ed Hudson's motorboat run to Lee's Ferry. The crew, including Otis Marston and Willie Taylor, returned in their hard-hulled, Higgins-type *Esmeralda II* to Lake Mead.

Mile 225.7
Diamond Creek
Map 21

In December 1857, Joseph Ives, leading an upriver expedition under the direction of the War Department, departed from the mouth of the Colorado. One purpose of the expedition was to determine how far upstream a steamboat could travel. After nearly destroying their 54-foot *Explorer* at the mouth of Black Canyon, 20 miles below what is now Hoover Dam, Ives and his company of fifty-four men left the river and explored eastward into the Grand Canyon region. Hualapai guides led the procession down Peach Springs Canyon. "The place grew wilder and grander," wrote Ives, as "the sides of the tortuous cañon became loftier, and before long we were hemmed in by walls two thousand feet high." Before dark, they camped where a clear stream joined the canyon. Ives named the stream Diamond River. That evening, a few explorers wandered down to the Colorado, becoming the first non-Indians on record to reach the floor of the Grand Canyon. Although impressed by the immensity of the "Big Cañon," Ives doubted the chasm would fulfill any human need:

The region is, of course, altogether valueless. It can be approached only from the south, and after entering it there is nothing to do but leave. Ours has been the first, and will doubtless be the last, party of whites to visit this profitless locality. It seems intended by nature that the Colorado river, along the greatest portion of its lonely and majestic way, shall be forever unvisited and undisturbed.

The next party of whites to see Diamond Creek was the malnourished Powell expedition in 1869, although the crew made no mention of the fact.

On October 7, 1871, George Montague Wheeler and his party of about twenty-seven departed the Grand Wash Cliffs area and began towing three flat-bottomed skiffs upriver toward Diamond Creek, over 50 thrilling rapid-filled miles. Wheeler, leader of this U.S. Geographical Survey west of the 100th Meridian, had already subjected his weary crew, including fourteen rebellious Mohave Indians, to a 140-mile up-drag from Camp Mohave. Now he intended to tow his boats up the same rapids Powell's earlier downriver expedition found so difficult. One boat was severely damaged and returned to Grand Wash. Rations became so short that, as a precaution against theft, Wheeler felt compelled to stuff what little food remained into his blanket pillow as the crew slept. Towing became "a thing very much to be dreaded" wrote Wheeler, and "each day seems like an age." Finally, after thirteen dreadful, backbreaking days, the party reached Diamond Creek, concluding this "masterpiece of successful exploring."

In 1884, J. H. Farlee built a small framed building with a porch, eight guest rooms, a small lobby, a kitchen, and a dining room. The structure was the first hotel at Grand Canyon and apparently was constructed on the site of Farlee's earlier tourist camp near the Peach Springs-Diamond Creek confluence.

Access to the hotel required a four-hour bruising ride, and although Farlee averaged about 100 guests a year, the establishment closed in 1889 as transportation to the South Rim improved.

Mile 237.0
Bessie and Glen
Hyde
Map 22

"I wonder if I shall ever wear pretty shoes again," said the petite, dark-haired Bessie Hyde before descending into the cold canyon in November 1928. In a homemade 20-foot scow, Bessie and her husband Glen traveled the turbulent stretch between Green River, Utah, and Bright Angel Creek. After spending time with Emery Kolb on the South Rim, the young couple returned to the river and resumed their honeymoon voyage. They were last seen at Hermit Rapid.

The next month, Emery and Ellsworth Kolb enlisted in the search for the Hydes. The brothers launched at Diamond Creek on Christmas Day, after repairing an abandoned, flat-bottomed derelict found along the river. They floated to where an aircraft had sited the Hydes' deserted scow. With its bowline snagged on the river bottom, the missing craft floated quietly in the eddy at Mile 237. Emery and Ellsworth removed Bessie's diary, a camera, a gun, and a guidebook. Later that day the brothers attempted Separation Rapid, capsized and lost a number of the Hydes' possessions. Bessie and Glen probably drowned at 232 Mile Rapid. Although her story ended sadly, Bessie became the first of an increasing number of women to operate a boat through the Grand Canyon.

Mile 239.5
Separation
Rapid
Map 23

August 28, 1869, marked the darkest day of the Powell expedition. After months of grueling labor and starvation, the crew encountered a rapid that had to be run yet seemed worse than any yet faced. Three crewmen—William Dunn, O. G. Howland, and Seneca Howland—expressed their desire to leave the river and strike out for the Mormon communities to the north. Powell spent a sleepless night struggling to decide whether to stay with the river or start walking. By morning the decision was reached: Dunn and the Howland brothers took their leave, and the remaining five river men remained with Powell. After a solemn parting—each party thinking the other was taking the dangerous course—Powell's two remaining boats (the *Emma Dean* had been abandoned at the rapid) successfully ran the rapid now remembered as Separation. The following day the river party safely emerged from the Grand Canyon. Dunn and the Howland brothers were probably killed by Indians, although their bodies were never recovered. By 1938 the encroaching waters of Lake Mead covered Separation Rapid, leaving its fury to folklore and the memories of very few.

After three arduous months the Powell expedition reached the Grand Wash Cliffs, the terminus of the Grand Canyon. "Now the danger is over, now the toil has ceased, now the gloom has disappeared, now the firmament is bounded only by the horizon," wrote Powell. The following day the expedition arrived at the mouth of the Virgin River where three Mormon settlers greeted them. The journey had ended.

Mile 278.0
Grand Wash Cliffs
Map 26

✕

Allen, David. "A Daring Voyage Down the Colorado." *The Wide World Magazine* 22 (November 1908): 65-72.

Baker, Pearl. *Trail on the Water*. Boulder, Colorado: Pruett Press, 1970.

Beer, Bill. "We Swam the Colorado." *Collier's Magazine* 136 (August 5, 1955): 19-20.

Billingsly, George H. "Mining in the Grand Canyon," in *Geology of the Grand Canyon*, ed. by William Breed and Evelyn Roat. Flagstaff, Arizona: Museum of Northern Arizona and Grand Canyon, Grand Canyon Natural History Association, 1974.

_____, and William J. Breed. "Mississipian Nautiloids of the Grand Canyon." *Plateau* 48 (1976): 67-69.

Birdseye, Claude H. "Exploration in the Grand Canyon." *Reclamation Era*, 28 (August 1938): 170.

_____, and Raymond Moore. "A Boat Voyage through the Grand Canyon of the Colorado." *The Geological Review* 14 (April 1924): 177-196.

Chavez, Fray Angelico, ed., and Ted J. Warner, trans. *The Dominquez-Escalante Journal*. Provo: Brigham Young University Press, 1976.

Clark, Neil M. "Fastwater Man." *Saturday Evening Post* 218 (May 1946): 30-31, 148.

Cooley, M.E., B.N. Alridge, and R.C. Euler. *Effects of the Catastrophic Flood of December 1966, North Rim Area, Eastern Grand Canyon, Arizona*. U.S.G.S. Professional Paper 980. Washington: Government Printing Office.

Cushing, Frank Hamilton. *The Nation of Willows*. Flagstaff, Arizona: Northland Press, 1965.

Darrah, William C., ed. Biographical sketches and original documents of the first Powell expedition of 1869. *Utah Historical Quarterly* 15 (1947): 1-148.

Davis, Daniel E. *A Resume of the Scientific Values and Interpretive Potential of the Little Colorado and its Environs*, Unpublished MS in the reference library, Grand Canyon National Park.

Dellenbaugh, Frederick S. *A Canyon Voyage*. New Haven: Yale University Press, 1926.

_____. *The Romance of the Colorado River*. Chicago: Rio Grande Press, 1965.

Dobyns, Henry F., and Robert C. Euler. *The Navajo People*. Phoenix: Indian Tribal Series, 1972.

_____ and _____. *The Walapai People*. Phoenix: Indian Tribal Series, 1976.

Eddy, Clyde. *Down the World's Most Dangerous River*. New York: Frederick Stokes, 1929.

Euler, Robert C. *Southern Paiute Ethnohistory*. University of Utah Anthropological Papers No. 78. Salt Lake City, Utah, April 1966.

_____. "Willow Figurines from Arizona." *Natural History* 85 (March 1966).

_____. "The Canyon Dwellers." *The American West* 4 (May 1967): 22-27, 67-71.

_____. *The Paiute People*. Phoenix: Indian Tribal Series, 1972.

Freeman, Lewis R. "Surveying the Grand Canyon of the Colorado." *National Geographic Magazine* 45 (May 1924): 472-532.

Goldwater, Barry. *Delightful Journey*. Tempe, Arizona: Arizona Historical Foundation, 1970.

Granger, Byrd H. *Grand Canyon Place Names*. Tucson: University of Arizona Press, 1960.

Hamilton, Joyce. *Whitewater*. Christchurch, New Zealand: Caxton Press, 1963.

Hillers, Jack. *"Photographed all the Best Scenery": Jack Hillers' Diary of the Powell Expeditions, 1871-75*, ed. by Don Fowler. Salt Lake City, Utah: University of Utah Press, 1972.

Hirst, Stephen. *Life in A Narrow Place*. New York: David McKay, 1976.

Hoffman, John. "The Grand Canyon: Horrid Abyss, Wondrous Titan of Chasms," in *National Parkways: A Photographic and Comprehensive Guide to Grand Canyon National Park*. Casper, Wyoming: Worldwide Research and Publishing Company, 1977.

Hughes, Donald J. *In the House of Light and Stone: A Human History of the Grand Canyon*. Grand Canyon, Arizona: Grand Canyon Natural History Association, 1978.

Ives, Ronald L. "Bert Loper—The Last Chapter." *The Journal of Arizona History* 17 (Spring 1976): 49-54.

Jennings, Jesse D. *Prehistory of North America*. San Francisco: McGraw-Hill Book Company, 1974.

Jones, Ann Trinkle and Robert C. Euler. *A Sketch of Grand Canyon Prehistory*. Grand Canyon, Arizona: Grand Canyon Natural History Association, 1979.

Judge, Joseph. "Retracing John Wesley Powell's Historic Voyage Down the Grand Canyon." *National Geographic Magazine* 135 (May 1969): 668-713.

Kolb, Ellsworth L. *Through the Grand Canyon from Wyoming to Mexico*. New York: The MacMillian Company, 1914.

———— and Emery Kolb. "Experiences in the Grand Canyon." *National Geographic Magazine* 26 (August 1914): 99-184.

Kroeber, Alfred Louis, ed. "Walapai Ethnography." *Memoirs of the American Anthropological Association*, 42, Contributions from the Laboratory of Anthropology I, 1935.

Lavender, David. *River Runners of the Grand Canyon*. Tucson: University of Arizona Press and the Grand Canyon Natural History Association, 1985.

Manners, Robert A., Henry Dobyns, and Robert C. Euler. *Havasupai Indians: An Ethnohistorical Report*. New York and London: Garland Publishing, Inc., 1974.

Marston, Otis "Dock". *Colorado River Journals and Diaries*. MS in Reference Library, Grand Canyon National Park.

————. "River Runners: Fastwater Navigation." *Utah Historical Quarterly* 28 (July 1960): 300-307.

————. "Who Named the Grand Canyon?" *The Pacific Historian* 3 (Summer 1968): 4-8.

————. "Separation Mark." *The Journal of Arizona History* 17 (Spring 1976): 14-15.

Nash, Roderick. "Conservation and the Colorado," in *The Grand Colorado: The Story of a River and its Canyons*, ed. by T.H. Watkins. Palo Alto, California: American West Publishing Co., 1969.
———. *Grand Canyon of the Colorado*. San Francisco: Sierra Club, 1970.

Nims, Franklin A. *The Photographer and the River, 1889-1890: The Colorado Canyon Diary of Franklin Nims*, ed. by Dwight L. Smith. Santa Fe: Stagecoach Press, 1962.

Powell, John Wesley. *Exploration of the Colorado River and Its Tributaries*. Washington: Government Printing Office, 1875.
———. *Exploration of the Colorado River and Its Canyons*. New York: Dover Publications, Inc., 1961.

Reilly, P.T. "How Deadly is Big Red." *Utah Historical Quarterly* 37 (1969): 244-260.

Rusho, W.L. and C. Gregory Crampton. *Desert River Crossing: Historic Lee's Ferry on the Colorado River*. Salt Lake City, Utah: Peregrine Smith, 1975.

Schwartz, Douglas W. "An Archaeological Survey of Nankoweap Canyon, Grand Canyon National Park." *American Antiquity* 28 (January 1963): 289-302.
———. "Nankoweap to Unkar: An Archaeological Survey of the Upper Grand Canyon." *American Antiquity* 30 (1965).
———, Richard C. Chapman, and Jane Kepp. *Archaeology of the Grand Canyon: Unkar Delta*. Santa Fe, New Mexico: School of American Research Press, 1980.

Spearman, Rupert P. "Lone Boatman Navigates the Colorado River." *Reclamation Era* 28 (February 1938): 51.

Spier, Leslie. *Havasupai Ethnography*. New York: Anthropological Papers of the American Museum of Natural History, Vol. 29, No. 3, 1928.

Stanton, Robert. "Engineering with a Camera in the Canyons of the Colorado." *The Cosmopolitan* 15 (Aug 1893): 249-297.

———. *Down the Colorado*, ed. by Dwight L. Smith. Norman, Oklahoma: University of Oklahoma Press, 1968.

Stone, Julius F. *Canyon Country: The Romance of a Drop of Water and a Grain of Sand*. New York: G.P. Putman's Sons, 1932.

Watkins, T.H., ed. *The Grand Colorado: The Story of a River and its Canyons*. Palo Alto, California: American West Publishing Company, 1969.

Wheeler, George M. *Report Upon United States Geographical Surveys West of the One Hundredth Meridian: Geographical Report*. Washington, D.C.: Government Printing Office, 1889.

Yochelson, E. L., "Charles D. Walcott—America's Pioneer in Precambrian Paleontology and Stratigraphy,." in *History of Concepts in Precambrian Geology*, Geologic Association of Canada Special Paper 19, edited by W. O. Kupsch and W. A. S. Sarjeant (Toronto: Geological Association of Canada Publications, 1976), pp. 261–292. See also Charles D. Walcott, "Report of Charles D. Walcott (Fieldwork near Eureka, Nevada, and in Eastern Part of Grand Canyon of the Colorado in Arizona)," in *Administrative Reports of the Chiefs of Divisions: United States Geological Survey, 4th Annual Report, 1882–83* (Washington: Government Printing Office, 1184), pp. 44–48.

MAPS

Maps based on U.S.G.S. topographical maps
Approximate scale: 1:24,000
Orientation of maps varies. North is indicated on each map.
Heavy dashed lines: park and reservation boundaries
Numbers in blue: miles below Lee's Ferry

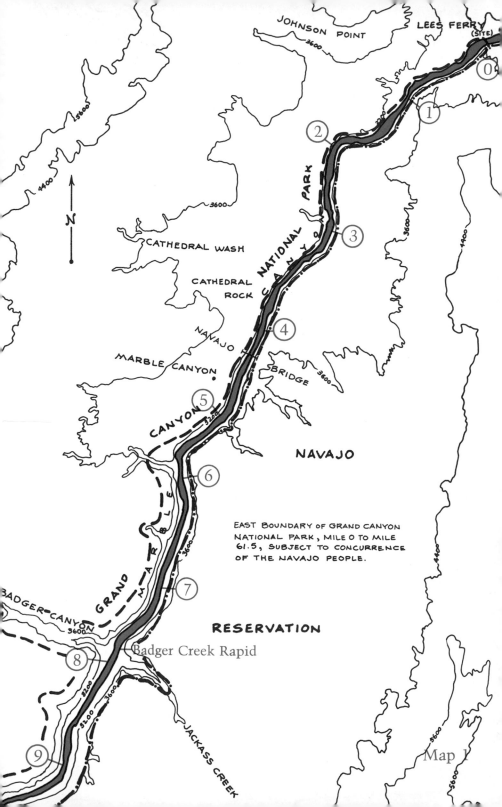

JOHNSON POINT

LEES FERRY (SITE)

CATHEDRAL WASH

CATHEDRAL ROCK

NAVAJO

MARBLE CANYON

NAVAJO BRIDGE

NATIONAL PARK

GRAND CANYON

EAST BOUNDARY OF GRAND CANYON NATIONAL PARK, MILE 0 TO MILE 61.5, SUBJECT TO CONCURRENCE OF THE NAVAJO PEOPLE.

NAVAJO

RESERVATION

BADGER CANYON

Badger Creek Rapid

JACKASS CREEK

Map 1

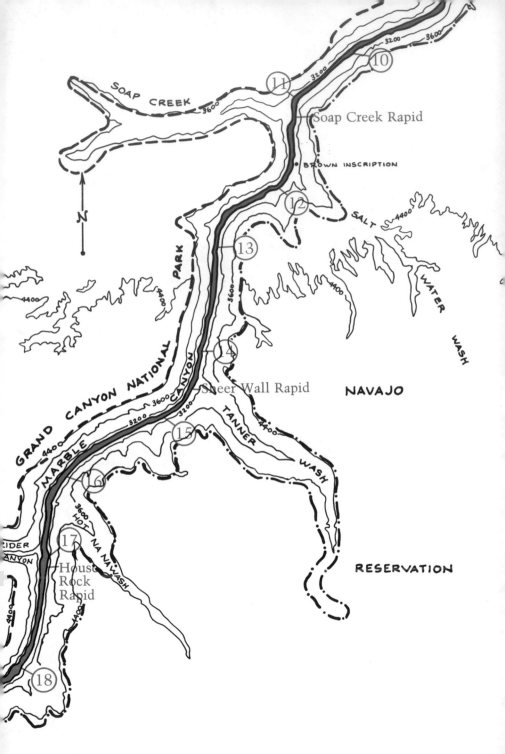

Map 2

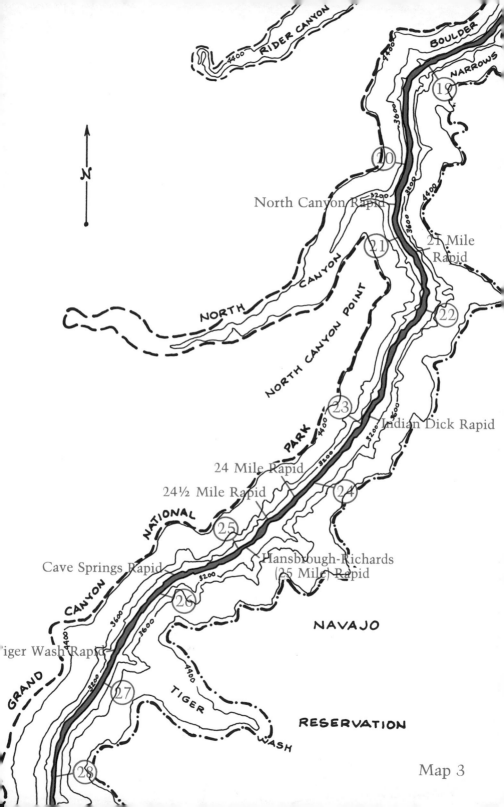

Map 3

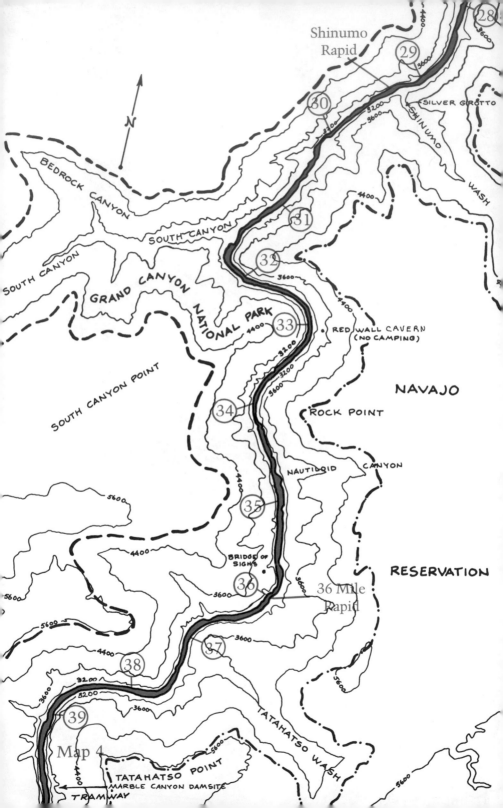

N

Shinumo
Rapid

SILVER GROTTO

SHINUMO WASH

BEDROCK CANYON

SOUTH CANYON

SOUTH CANYON

GRAND CANYON NATIONAL PARK

SOUTH CANYON POINT

RED WALL CAVERN
(NO CAMPING)

NAVAJO

ROCK POINT

NAUTILOID CANYON

RESERVATION

BRIDGE OF SIGHS

36 Mile
Rapid

Map 4

TATAHATSO WASH

TATAHATSO POINT
MARBLE CANYON DAMSITE
TRAMWAY

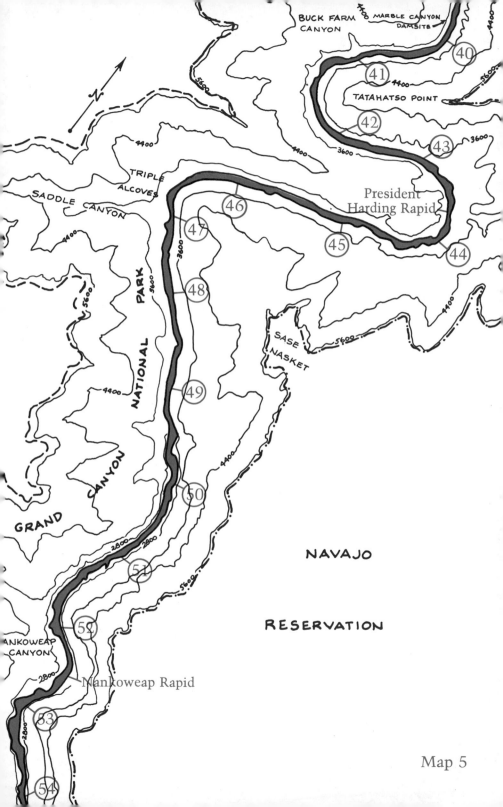

BUCK FARM
CANYON

MARBLE CANYON
DAMSITE

40

41

TATAHATSO POINT

42

43

TRIPLE
ALCOVES

SADDLE CANYON

President
Harding Rapid

46

47

45

44

48

SASE
NASKET

NATIONAL PARK

49

50

GRAND CANYON

NAVAJO

RESERVATION

51

52

NANKOWEAP
CANYON

Nankoweap Rapid

53

54

Map 5

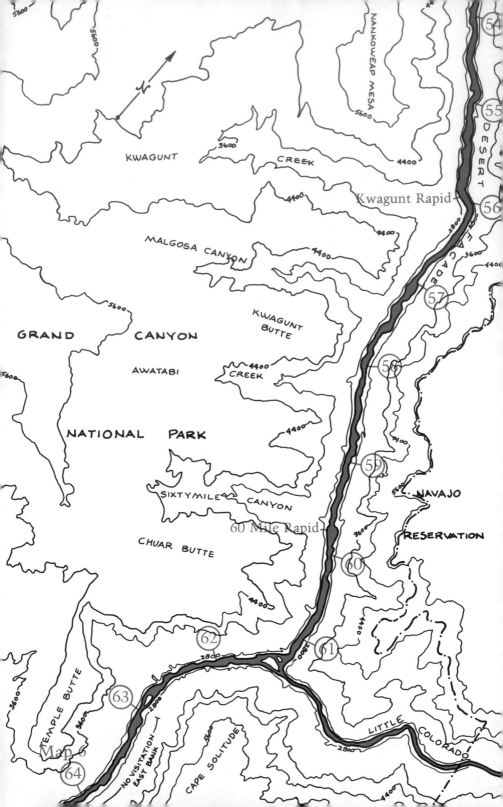

54

55

56

57

56

59

60

61

62

63

64

DESERT FACADE

NANKOWEAP MESA

5600

KWAGUNT

CREEK

4400

Kwagunt Rapid

4400

4400

MALGOSA CANYON

4400

5600

3600

KWAGUNT BUTTE

GRAND CANYON

AWATABI

4400

CREEK

NATIONAL PARK

4400

4400

SIXTYMILE CANYON

NAVAJO

RESERVATION

60 Mile Rapid

CHUAR BUTTE

4400

4400

2800

TEMPLE BUTTE

3600

Map 6

NO VISITATION EAST BANK

2800

2800

LITTLE COLORADO

CAPE SOLITUDE

2800

4400

3600

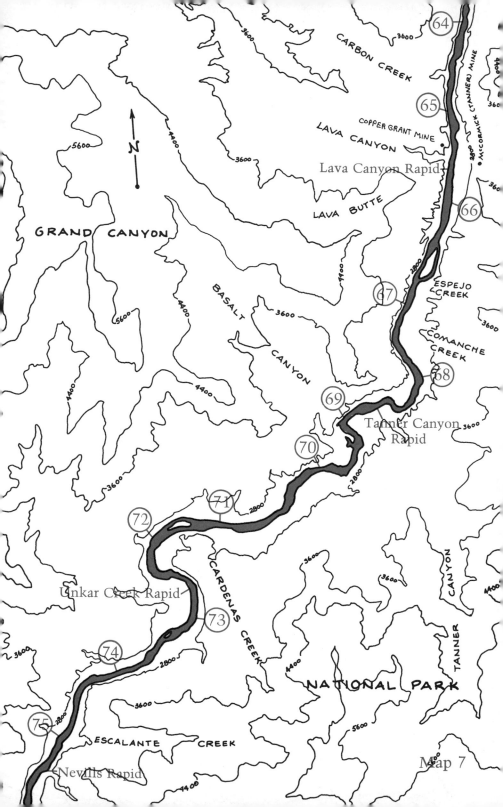

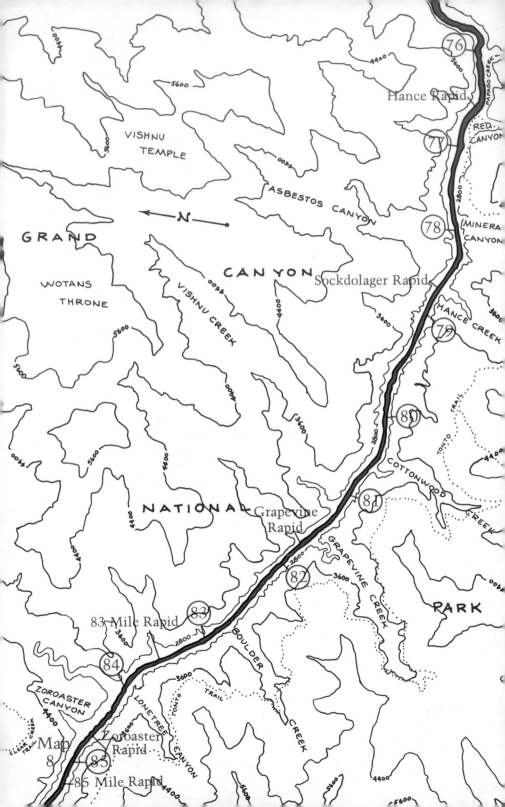

VISHNU
TEMPLE

ASBESTOS CANYON

← N →

GRAND

CANYON

Sockdolager Rapid

WOTANS
THRONE

VISHNU CREEK

HANCE CREEK

PAPAGO CREEK

RED
CANYON

MINERAL
CANYON

Hance Rapid

76

77

78

79

80

TONTO TRAIL

COTTONWOOD CREEK

NATIONAL

Grapevine
Rapid

81

GRAPEVINE CREEK

PARK

82

83-Mile Rapid

83

84

BOULDER CREEK

TONTO TRAIL

ZOROASTER
CANYON

LONETREE CANYON

TONTO TRAIL

CLEAR CREEK

TRAIL CREEK

Map
8

Zoroaster
Rapid

85

85-Mile Rapid

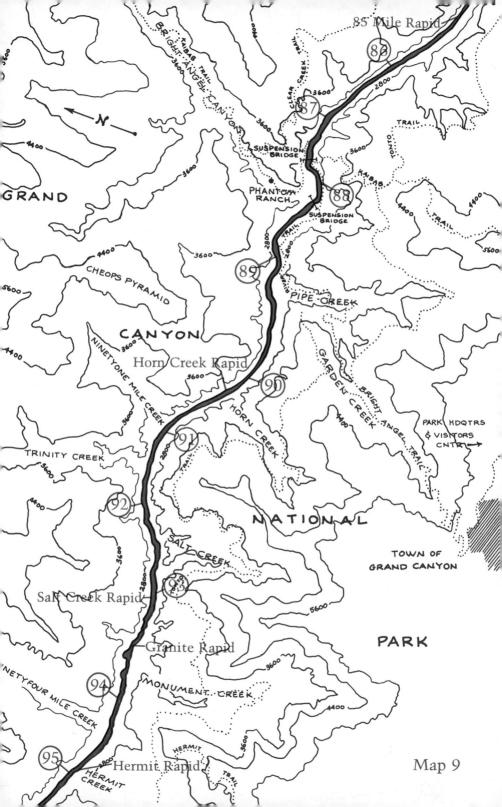

85 Mile Rapid

86

KAIBAB TRAIL

CLEAR CREEK TRAIL

BRIGHT ANGEL CANYON

3600

2800

87

3600

N

4400

TONTO TRAIL

3600

SUSPENSION BRIDGE

KAIBAB TRAIL

TRAIL

GRAND

3600

PHANTOM RANCH

88

4400

5600

SUSPENSION BRIDGE

CHEOPS PYRAMID

3600

89

2800

PIPE CREEK

CANYON

3600

Horn Creek Rapid

GARDEN CREEK

BRIGHT ANGEL TRAIL

PARK HDQTRS & VISITORS CNTR

5600

NINETYONE MILE CREEK

3600

90

HORN CREEK

4400

91

2800

TRINITY CREEK

3600

N A T I O N A L

TOWN OF GRAND CANYON

4400

92

3600

SALT CREEK

Salt Creek Rapid

93

PARK

5600

Granite Rapid

3600

NINETYFOUR MILE CREEK

94

MONUMENT CREEK

4400

2800

HERMIT TRAIL

95

Hermit Rapid

HERMIT CREEK

Map 9

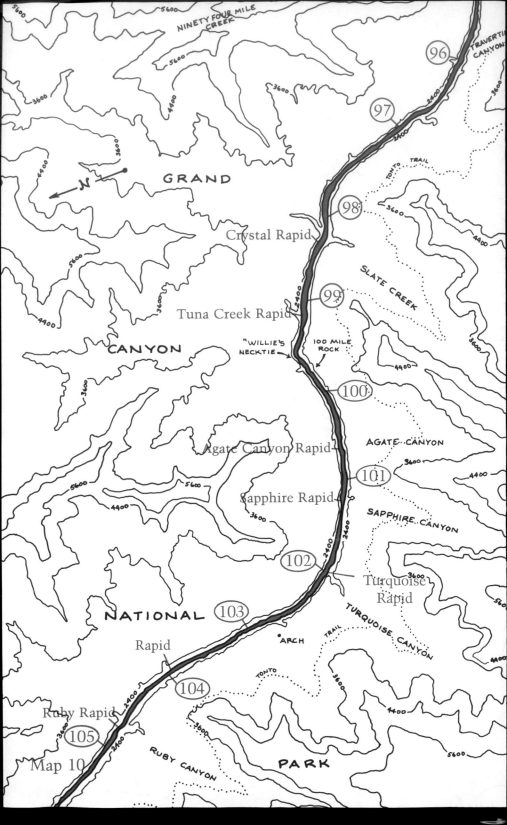

NINETY FOUR MILE CREEK

96

97

TRAVERTINE CANYON

N

GRAND

98

Crystal Rapid

TONTO TRAIL

SLATE CREEK

99

Tuna Creek Rapid

"WILLIE'S NECKTIE"

100 MILE ROCK

CANYON

100

AGATE CANYON

Agate Canyon Rapid

101

Sapphire Rapid

SAPPHIRE CANYON

102

Turquoise Rapid

NATIONAL

103

Rapid

ARCH

TRAIL

TURQUOISE CANYON

TONTO

104

Ruby Rapid

105

RUBY CANYON

PARK

Map 10

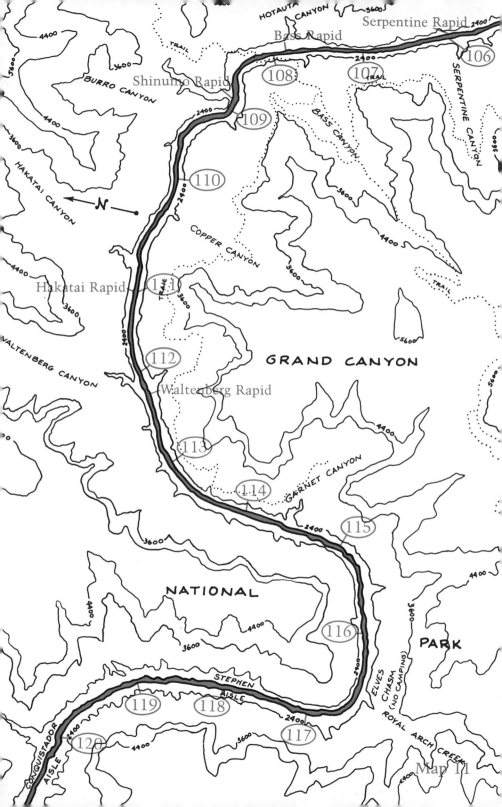

Serpentine Rapid

Bass Rapid

HOTAUTA CANYON

3600

2400

(106)

(108)

(107)

TRAIL

Shinumo Rapid

BURRO CANYON

3600

4400

(109)

2400

SERPENTINE CANYON

3600

4400

BASS CANYON

TRAIL

3600

(110)

2400

COPPER CANYON

N

HAKATAI CANYON

4400

4400

3600

TRAIL

5600

Hakatai Rapid

(111)

2400

3600

GRAND CANYON

WALTENBERG CANYON

4400

(112)

3600

5600

Waltenberg Rapid

2400

(113)

4400

GARNET CANYON

(114)

(115)

2400

3600

4400

NATIONAL

4400

(116)

3600

PARK

4400

STEPHEN

ELVES CHASM (NO CAMPING)

(119)

AISLE

(118)

ROYAL ARCH CREEK

CONQUISTADOR

2400

(120)

(117)

AISLE

4400

3600

4400

Map 11

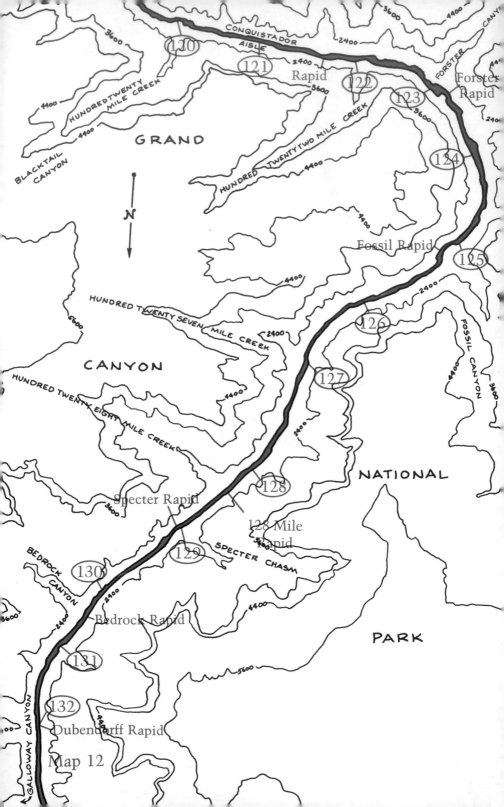

CONQUISTADOR AISLE

120

121

Rapid

122

123

Forster
Rapid

FORSTER

124

HUNDRED TWENTY MILE CREEK

BLACKTAIL CANYON

GRAND

N

HUNDRED TWENTYTWO MILE CREEK

Fossil Rapid

125

HUNDRED TWENTY SEVEN MILE CREEK

126

FOSSIL CANYON

CANYON

127

HUNDRED TWENTY EIGHT MILE CREEK

NATIONAL

128

Specter Rapid

128 Mile
Rapid

SPECTER CHASM

129

BEDROCK CANYON

130

PARK

Bedrock Rapid

131

132

GALLOWAY CANYON

Dubendorff Rapid

Map 12

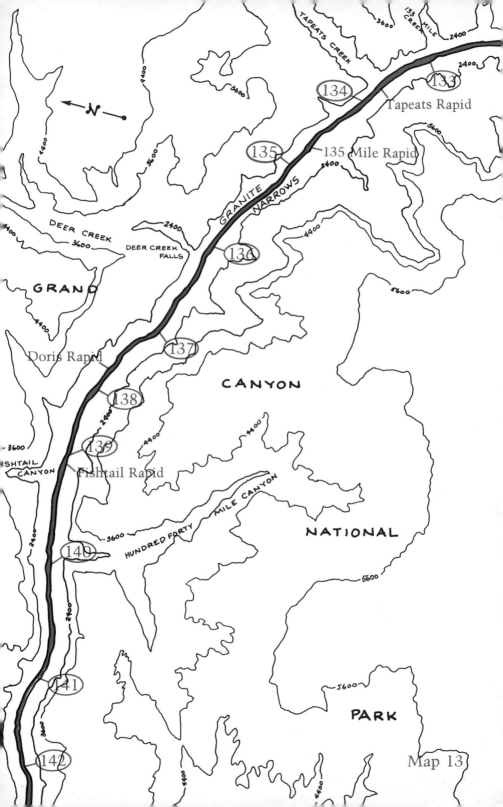

N

133 MILE CREEK

TAPEATS CREEK

2400

3600

2400

134

133

Tapeats Rapid

3600

135

135 Mile Rapid

GRANITE NARROWS

2400

3600

DEER CREEK

2400

3600

DEER CREEK FALLS

136

4400

4400

4400

4400

5600

GRAND

4400

4400

CANYON

137

Doris Rapid

138

4400

4400

3600

139

SHTAIL CANYON

Fishtail Rapid

2400

HUNDRED FORTY MILE CANYON

NATIONAL

4400

3600

140

2400

3600

5600

5600

141

3600

PARK

5600

Map 13

142

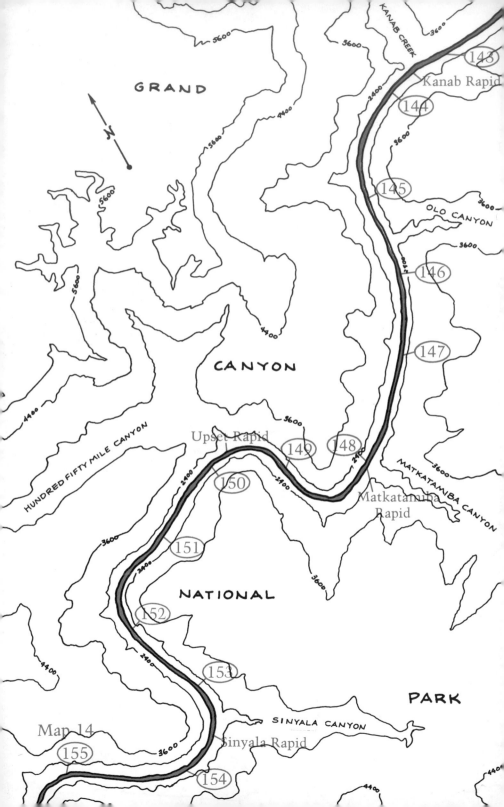

GRAND

CANYON

NATIONAL

PARK

KANAB CREEK

Kanab Rapid

OLO CANYON

MATKATAMIBA CANYON

Matkatamiba
Rapid

Upset Rapid

HUNDRED FIFTY MILE CANYON

SINYALA CANYON

Sinyala Rapid

Map 14

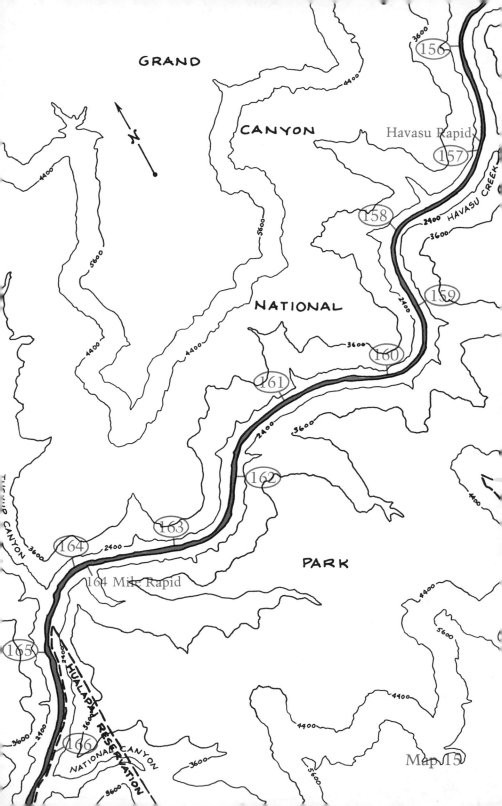

GRAND

CANYON

NATIONAL

PARK

Havasu Rapid

164 Mile Rapid

156
157
158
159
160
161
162
163
164
165
166

4400
3600
2400
HAVASU CREEK
3600
5600
4400
4400
3600
2400
4400
3600
2400
4400
4400
5600
4400
5600
3600
3600
2400
3600
2400
HUALAPAI RESERVATION
NATIONAL CANYON
3600
2400
TUCKUP CANYON

N

Map 15

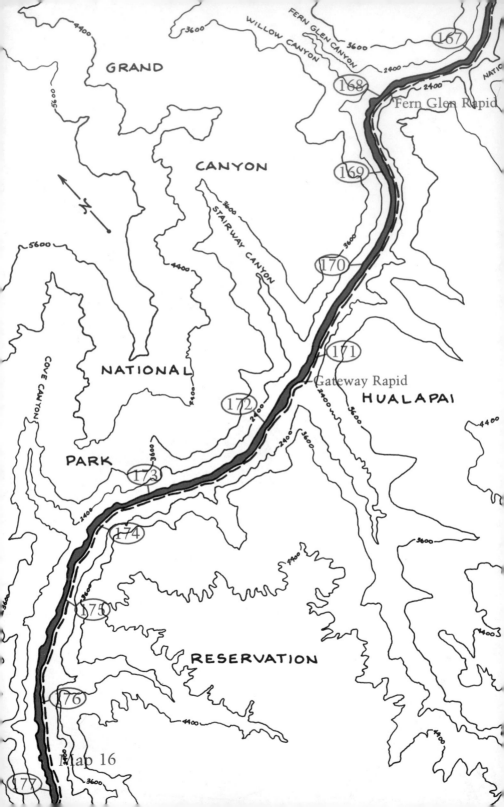

Map 16

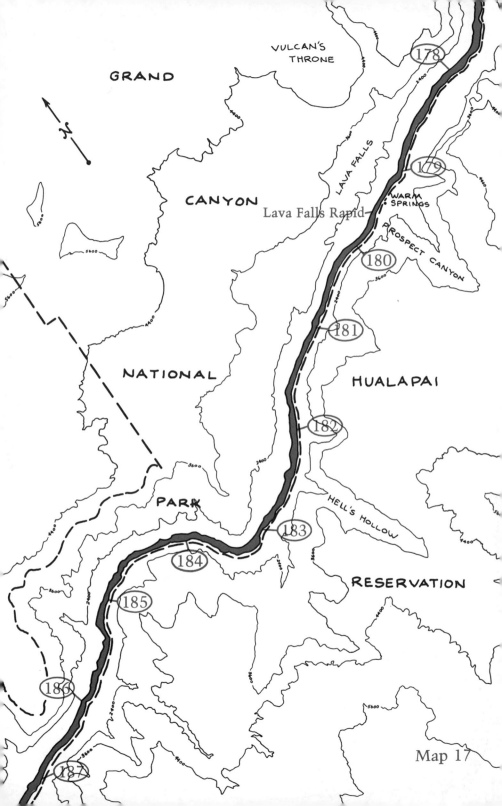

GRAND

VULCAN'S
THRONE

CANYON

Lava Falls Rapid

NATIONAL

HUALAPAI

PARK

HELL'S HOLLOW

RESERVATION

LAVA FALLS

WARM
SPRINGS

PROSPECT CANYON

178

179

180

181

182

183

184

185

186

187

Map 17

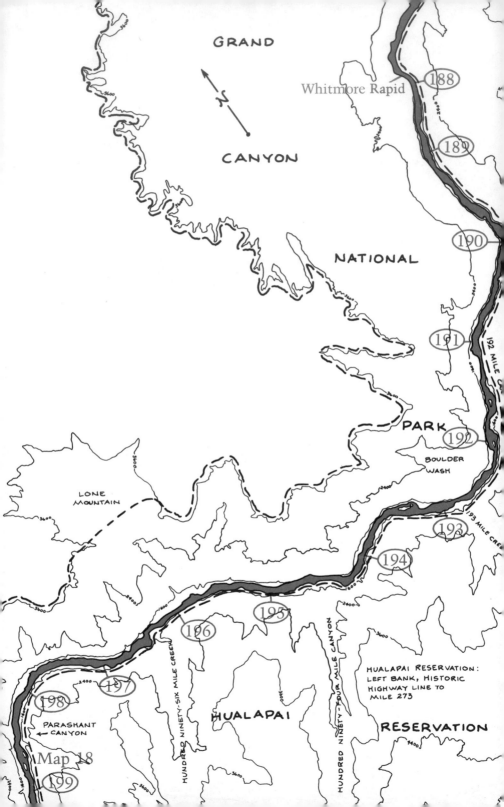

GRAND

CANYON

NATIONAL

PARK

Whitmore Rapid

188

189

190

191

192 MILE CANYON

192

BOULDER
WASH

193 MILE CREEK

193

194

195

196

197

198

199

LONE
MOUNTAIN

PARASHANT
← CANYON

Map 18

HUNDRED NINETY-SIX MILE CREEK

HUNDRED NINETY-FOUR MILE CANYON

HUALAPAI

HUALAPAI RESERVATION:
LEFT BANK, HISTORIC
HIGHWAY LINE TO
MILE 273

RESERVATION

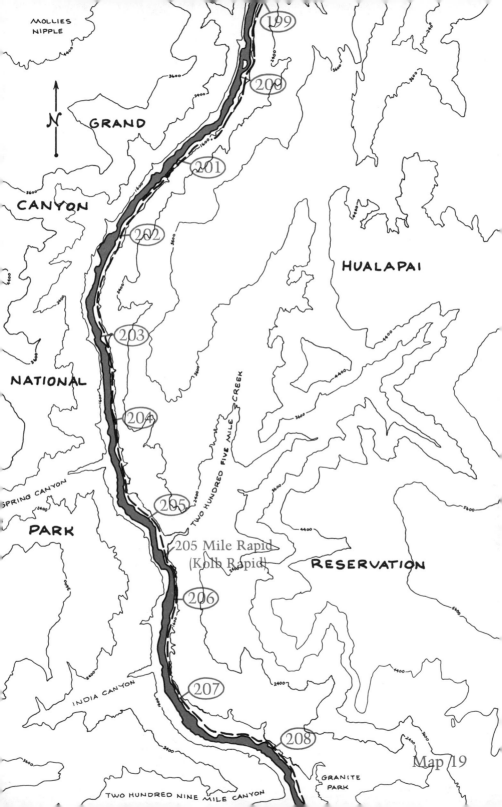

MOLLIES NIPPLE

N

GRAND

CANYON

HUALAPAI

NATIONAL

TWO HUNDRED FIVE MILE CREEK

SPRING CANYON

PARK

205 Mile Rapid
(Kolb Rapid)

RESERVATION

INDIA CANYON

GRANITE PARK

Map 19

TWO HUNDRED NINE MILE CANYON

199

200

201

202

203

204

205

206

207

208

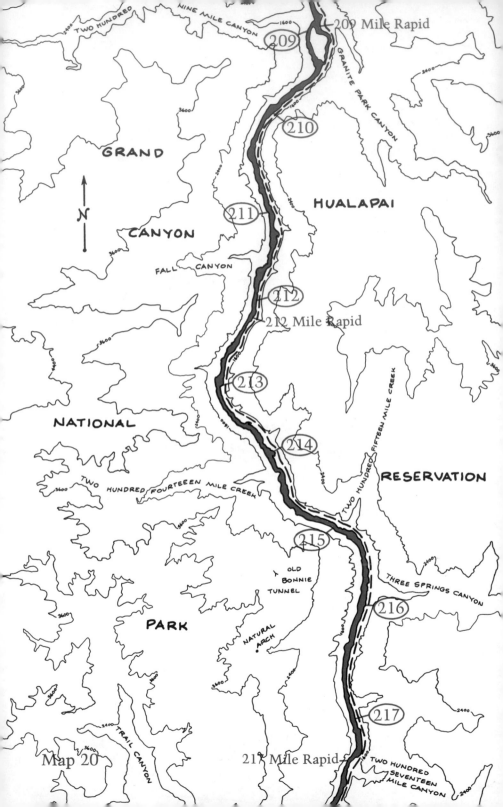

209 Mile Rapid

209

NINE MILE CANYON

TWO HUNDRED

1600

GRANITE PARK CANYON

210

GRAND

N

CANYON

HUALAPAI

211

FALL CANYON

212

212 Mile Rapid

NATIONAL

213

214

RESERVATION

TWO HUNDRED FOURTEEN MILE CREEK

TWO HUNDRED FIFTEEN MILE CREEK

215

OLD BONNIE TUNNEL

THREE SPRINGS CANYON

216

NATURAL ARCH

PARK

217

TRAIL CANYON

Map 20

217 Mile Rapid

TWO HUNDRED SEVENTEEN MILE CANYON

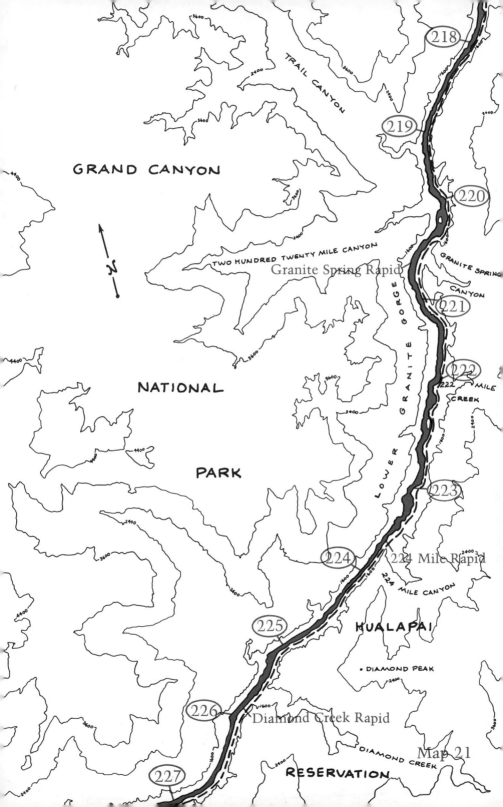

GRAND CANYON

TRAIL CANYON

218

219

220

NATIONAL

TWO HUNDRED TWENTY MILE CANYON

Granite Spring Rapid

GRANITE SPRING CANYON

221

222 MILE CREEK

222

223

PARK

224 Mile Rapid

224

224 MILE CANYON

HUALAPAI

225

• DIAMOND PEAK

226

Diamond Creek Rapid

Map 21

227

DIAMOND CREEK

RESERVATION

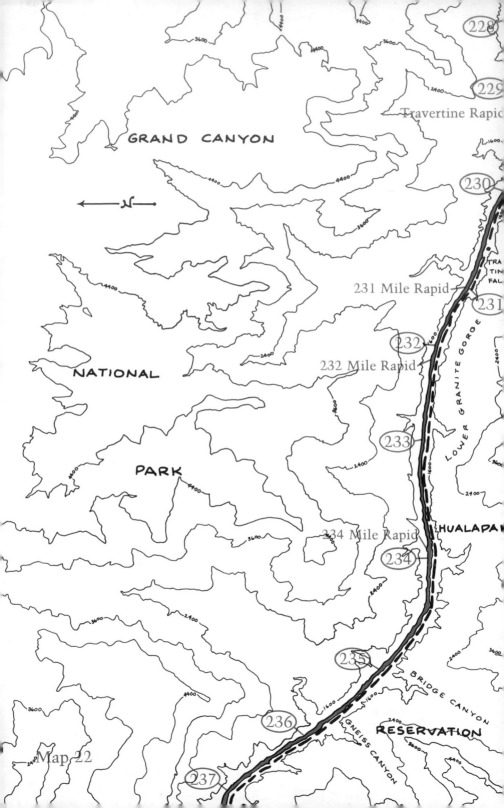

GRAND CANYON

← N →

228

229

Travertine Rapid

230

TRA
TIN
FAL

231 Mile Rapid

231

232

232 Mile Rapid

233

234 Mile Rapid

234

HUALAPAI

LOWER GRANITE GORGE

235

BRIDGE CANYON

236

RESERVATION

237

GNEISS CANYON

NATIONAL

PARK

Map 22

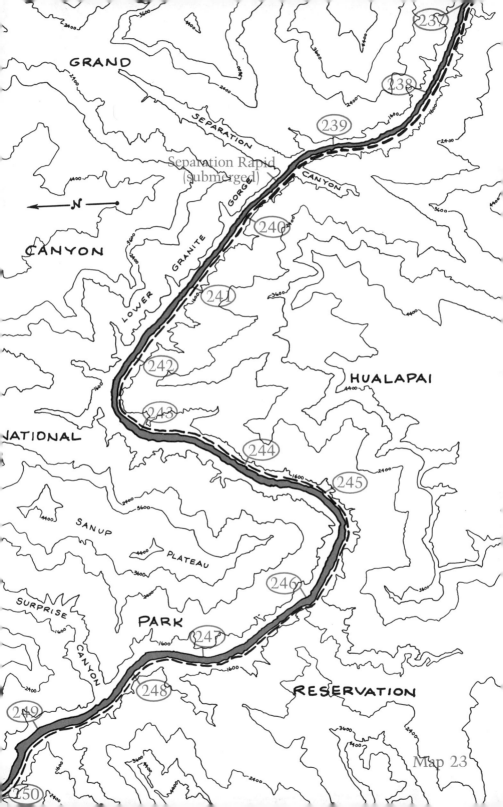

GRAND

SEPARATION

Separation Rapid
(submerged)

CANYON

N

CANYON

LOWER GRANITE GORGE

HUALAPAI

NATIONAL

SANUP

PLATEAU

SURPRISE

PARK

CANYON

RESERVATION

Map 23

237
238
239
240
241
242
243
244
245
246
247
248
249
250

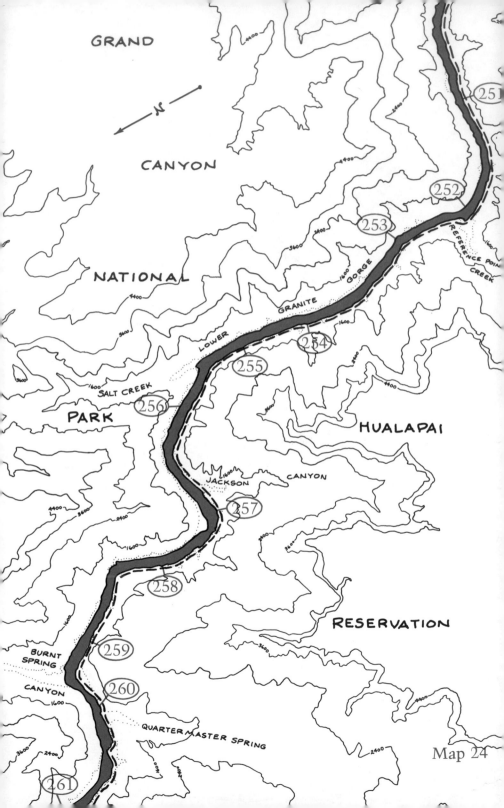

GRAND

CANYON

NATIONAL

PARK

251

252

253

REFERENCE POINT CREEK

GRANITE GORGE

LOWER

254

255

SALT CREEK

256

HUALAPAI

JACKSON CANYON

257

258

RESERVATION

BURNT SPRING

259

260

CANYON

QUARTERMASTER SPRING

261

Map 24

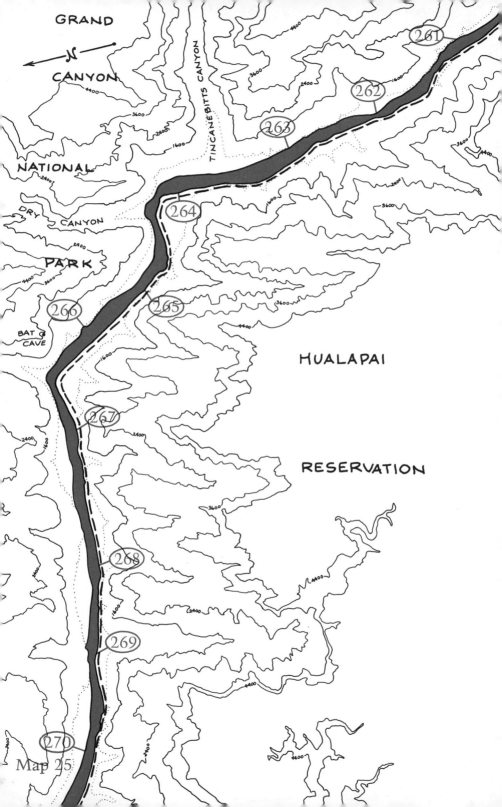

GRAND

CANYON

NATIONAL

DRY CANYON

PARK

BAT CAVE

TINCANEBITTS CANYON

261

262

263

264

265

266

267

268

269

270

Map 25

HUALAPAI

RESERVATION

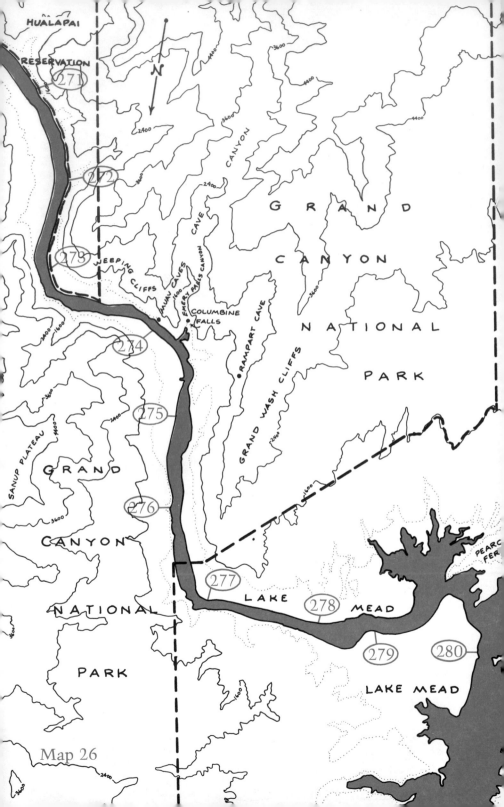

HUALAPAI

RESERVATION

271

N

272

273

WEEPING CLIFFS

CANYON

CAVE

HUALAPAI CAVES

EMERY FALLS CANYON

COLUMBINE FALLS

274

RAMPART CAVE

GRAND

CANYON

NATIONAL

PARK

GRAND WASH CLIFFS

275

SANUP PLATEAU

GRAND

276

CANYON

277

LAKE

278

MEAD

279

PEARCE FER

280

NATIONAL

LAKE MEAD

PARK

Map 26